In S̶e̶a̶r̶c̶h̶ ̶o̶f̶.

Significance

Why YOU Are
Important to God

To! Olivia,
God Bless you!
Bishop Ray
3/24/2024
Psalm 27

by

Ray Llarena

Unless otherwise noted, all Scripture references are from the Authorized King James Version of the Bible. References marked NKJ are from the New King James Version of the Bible copyright © 1979, 1980, 1982 by Thomas Nelson, Inc., Nashville, Tennessee.

This book was originally published under the title *In Search of Significance*.

McDougal Publishing is a ministry of The McDougal Foundation, Inc., a Maryland nonprofit corporation dedicated to spreading the Gospel of the Lord Jesus Christ to as many people as possible in the shortest time possible.

Published by:

McDougal Publishing
P.O. Box 3595
Hagerstown, MD   21742-3595
www.mcdougalpublishing.com

ISBN 1-58158-046-0
(Formerly ISBN 1-884369-67-7)

Printed in the United States of America
For Worldwide Distribution

There be four things which are little upon the earth, but they are exceeding wise: the ants are a people not strong, yet they prepare their meat in the summer; the conies are but a feeble folk, yet make they their houses in the rocks; the locusts have no king, yet go they forth all of them by bands; the spider taketh hold with her hands, and is in kings' palaces.

Proverbs 30:24-28

DEDICATION

I dedicate this book to all those who have felt their insignificance and have been convinced that they would never accomplish anything of lasting value in life, to those who have not yet tapped into their God-given abilities because the devil has lied to them and told them that they would never amount to anything.

You are so significant to God that He sent Jesus Christ to die for you, and He desires to make you part of His great Church and to use you to reveal His glory and majesty to all the world.

CONTENTS

INTRODUCTION

When God created us, He put within us the ability to be exactly what He desires us to be. Each of us has been created with a purpose, a plan and a destiny, and that purpose and plan and destiny are great.

We can be what we want to be only if we allow God to be what He wants to be in us. When this is our determination, nothing can hold us back in life. We will succeed at whatever we set our minds to.

Satan tries to make us focus on our weaknesses, our lack of talents and our inabilities, rather than on our strengths. God wants us to focus on Him, on His greatness and on His great design for life. If we are willing to do things His way, the sky is the limit. Nothing will be impossible for us. This has proven to be true in my own life.

I was born into humble circumstances in the Philippines. As I grew up, however, I came to understand that God had called me to the ministry. Over the years that followed, I have been able to serve God in many ways.

At first I traveled all over my own country, holding evangelistic crusades, church revivals and seminars. I pioneered my first church and pastored it for two years with great success. Then, after having served as associate pastor of the largest church in our country (and the largest church in Asia at the time), God called my wife and me as missionaries to Guam.

After two fruitful years in Guam, the Lord opened the way for us to move to the United States. For the first eight years of our time here, I served as an assistant pastor in an Assembly of God church in San Francisco. The church gave me great liberty, and I was able to travel and minister in many parts of the world, while still enjoying a fruitful ministry to the people of that great city.

After that, I was called to pastor a church in Cheboygan, Michigan. This was an amazing turn of events because the only other Asians in the community were a Chinese doctor and his family and a Filipina lady married to an American serviceman. Most immigrant pastors serve among their own people, but God called us to pastor a totally Caucasian congregation. We knew that if God was calling us, He would give us the grace to fulfill His will, and He did — through three and a half wonderful years in that place.

Things went very well for us in Cheboygan. The church people bought us a lovely house, and we were able to acquire very good furniture and a fine automobile. We were more than comfortable.

After we had been in Cheboygan for several years, however, God spoke to our hearts to move back to the Philippines. We obeyed, returning to our county in 1984.

We sensed that if God was calling us to make such a drastic move, it was for a great purpose that would become obvious before much time had passed. God did great miracles in our midst. Today, we have thirty-five churches and more than one hundred ministers working with us all over the Philippines. In Manila, the capital city, we built a beautiful church and Christian school for students from kindergarten through twelfth grade. This beautiful edifice, a great leap of faith in such a poor country, stands as a monument to the greatness of God and has challenged many others.

During the time I was again living in the Philippines, I also ministered in Hong Kong, China and Vietnam.

After twelve years of ministry in the Philippines, things were going well, but in the spring of 1996, God called me to return to the United States to pastor the Faith Tabernacle Church in Chicago, Illinois. It was also not a Filipino congregation, but was made up of people from more than forty nationalities. It had a current membership of some four thousand and was forced to have four services on Sunday to get everyone in. As much as I hated to leave my beloved Philippines and the revival we were experiencing there, I knew that this was God's will for me. Although I still go back to minister in the Philippines several times a year and am doing missionary work in many other nations, Chicago has become my home.

When I say that God can take seemingly insignificant people and use them for His glory, you can know where I am coming from. I have lived this message and, therefore, I can now present it to you with great conviction and authority.

There are no insignificant creatures with God. YOU are important to Him.

Open your heart as we explore together His teachings in this area of self-worth and personal destiny and let God plant within your soul the seeds of greatness that will cause you to rise up from your present level of achievement and go forth to greatness in God.

Pastor Ray Llarena
Chicago, Illinois

PART ONE:

GOD'S SMALL
CREATURES

1

SMALL, BUT WISE

There be four things which are little upon the earth, but they are exceeding wise: the ants are a people not strong, yet they prepare their meat in the summer; the conies are but a feeble folk, yet make they their houses in the rocks; the locusts have no king, yet go they forth all of them by bands; the spider taketh hold with her hands, and is in kings' palaces.   Proverbs 30:24-28

The Bible puts forth these four small creatures as being exceedingly wise. None of them are strong animals, yet they are examples for us. They excel by their cunning and are wise in their own ways. Although they seem to be insignificant to man, they are not insignificant to God. And despite their small size, they are of no less value than any other creature.

But God is not preaching here to ants and spiders. He is showing us His greater purpose for our lives. If we can believe it, He is telling us that in the Body of Christ there are no insignificant members. We are all important to God. He counts each one precious.

Every member of the Body of Christ, no matter how unimportant he may seem to others, has a place in the program of God. And each will answer to God on the Day of Judgment for the things God has committed to him.

What animal is smaller and less important than the ant? If you were to see a lion, you would run away in fear. But if you see an ant, you don't worry about it. If you don't want him around, you simply squash him. He cannot strike back. Even if he bites you, it's usually just a momentary annoyance. He is a very insignificant creature.

Do you ever feel that you are insignificant? Maybe you feel that there is nothing you can do. Perhaps you have come to a place where you say, "I really want to serve the Lord, but I have no talent. I have no ability. If I could only be like that brother ... If I could just have that sister's talent, I would be more useful in the Kingdom of God." And so you become discouraged, believing you are not what you should be.

But think about it. If everyone was a musician,

who would preach? If everyone was an evangelist, who would minister to the needs of the sick? God created each of us in a very unique way. He made each of us for different purposes, with different ambitions to fulfill, with different plans to accomplish.

Together we form the Body of Christ. It is as each member accomplishes his purpose and fulfills his calling, together with the other members, that we accomplish and carry out God's desire, His plan, His purpose and His will in the earth.

Have others tried to discourage you? "You might as well give it up; you might as well quit. You'll never amount to anything. You have no talent, no energy to contribute. You have nothing to do in the Kingdom of God." It isn't surprising if you have heard these things, because Satan is out to discourage us every chance he can get. He wants us to believe that we really don't matter, that we are nothing and can do nothing in the Kingdom.

But that's the biggest lie you could ever receive. And the tragic thing is that in our churches today there are many people who accept that lie. They are sitting in the pews in their churches Sunday after Sunday, meeting after meeting, but they are not advancing in the Kingdom of God. They are not contributing to God's purposes.

Why not? Because they believe the lies of the enemy. They believe they are insignificant. They believe they are nothing, that there is nothing they can do, that they have no talents or abilities. They believe they have no gifts whatsoever to give into the Kingdom. But they are wrong!

Don't accept that lie. Don't allow yourself to believe that you are nothing. Satan wants to rob you of your future and keep you from participating in what God is doing. The devil doesn't want you to believe that you have a great future in God. What a liar he is!

If Satan can convince you that you are worthless, you will not prepare yourself for the future, for the great things God is about to do. If Satan can convince you that you can do nothing, you will not enter into what God is doing, nor will you obey the voice of the Lord as He calls you forth into ministry.

Instead of listening to those lies, know that you are somebody in God. Believe that you are important in Him. God created you with a purpose, with a reason, with a plan, with a destiny to fulfill. You might be insignificant in your own sight; you might be insignificant in the eyes of the people of the world; even some members of your family might think you'll never amount to much, but God didn't create any junk. He formed you as a unique creation. He has placed in you specific giftings, talents and abilities that you will need to perform the work He calls you to do. Know that you are special to God. You are important to Him. Believe it, receive it and act like you believe it, because it is true. You are the apple of God's eye.

We are not always as we appear to be. It is possible to seem insignificant while being exceedingly wise. It is possible to seem feeble and still be strong. It is possible to seem to have nothing and at the same time to have everything. It is possible to seem relatively uneducated, while flowing with godly wisdom. It is possible to seem ugly to men, yet possess unusual beauty.

Those things that seem to us to be so insignificant are important to God. These four animals are indeed *"little upon the earth,"* yet God Himself declares them to be *"exceeding wise."*

Have you ever looked down on someone and thought that person was not very important? Have you ever looked down on yourself? God doesn't do that. He created each one of us, and in His sight, all of us are important. We each have a part to play in the Kingdom of God. We each have a part in the unfolding of the plan of God for mankind through the ages.

It is time for each of us to lay hold of the promises of God. It is time to clarify our vision and find out what God has created us to do. It is time for the Church to begin to lay hold of her destiny. Paul wrote to the Ephesians:

For we are his workmanship, created in Christ Je-

sus unto good works, which God hath before or-
dained that we should walk in them.

Ephesians 2:10

God has already *"ordained"* the *"good works"* He has for you to do. He has things planned for your life. Everything is prepared and in place. All you need to do is to get a revelation of what God has for you to accomplish. When you lay hold of God's plan for your life, when you begin to see in your mind's eye all that He has prepared for you, you will no longer be satisfied to remain where you are in God. Instead, you will strive for greater things.

We must be careful not to look down on others but to see them as they are in Christ. We must look for the Christ formed in them, for His life shining forth through them. We are to encourage and stir up that life in one another. Only then will we be able to properly evaluate others, honoring them and loving them as Christ commanded.

What is often even more difficult for many of us is to properly evaluate ourselves. Sometimes, when I look in the mirror in the morning, I like what I see. But there are often times when I'm disgusted with my reflection.

One particular morning, I was running a little behind schedule and was afraid I would be late getting to the office. When I went to the bathroom and looked in the mirror, I didn't like what I saw. My hair was all twisted around, and since it's thinning, I could see more of the top of my head than I would have liked. "Lord," I sighed, "this is not good!" I would have to do something with my hair before I could leave the house.

But right away I heard the Lord respond, "I created you the way you are. Be happy exactly the way you are. Accept yourself as you are, because that is how I have formed you."

As I was thinking about that, He continued, "I created you for My own pleasure, and not for your own enjoyment."

Isn't that marvelous? God created us just as He pleased! He designed us and planned for our creation. He has made us for His own enjoyment, for His own pleasure, for His own glory, for His own desire.

And even creation was not enough. Not only did our Lord create us, but He also has redeemed us. He has washed us by His blood and written our names in the Lamb's Book of Life. He has transformed our natures so that we have passed from death unto life. The power of sin has been broken, and we have been set free. We are on our way to Heaven so that God might have pleasure in us, that our lives might give glory and honor to Him and that His Name might be exalted in this world.

Rightly do the four and twenty elders sing before the throne:

Thou art worthy, O Lord, to receive glory and

honour and power: for thou hast created all things,
and for thy pleasure they are and were created.

Revelation 4:11

There was something else that the Spirit spoke to me that morning. He said, "When I created you, I did not make a mistake. I purposefully made you the way you are." God is the wisest Architect, the greatest Designer. He designs our lives as they should be.

If we are wise, we will look to God's purposes for our existence. We will become participants in the Kingdom of God, allowing Him to use us according to His plan. And we will begin to realize that He has created everything about who we are, not just the parts of ourselves that we like.

Yes, there are problems sometimes. Perhaps we are physically out of shape. Perhaps we lack the skills necessary to use the artistic talents the Lord has blessed us with. So, we must take care of our bodies, train our intellects and perfect our talents. But it is the Lord who has made us, and we have been created for His pleasure.

David sang:

Know ye that the LORD he is God: it is he that
hath made us, and not we ourselves; we are his
people, and the sheep of his pasture.

Psalm 100:3

Don't allow the devil to belittle you, and don't belittle yourself. Don't criticize the handiwork of God.

Woe unto him that striveth with his Maker! Let
the potsherd strive with the potsherds of the earth.
Shall the clay say to him that fashioneth it, What
makest thou? or thy work, He hath no hands?
Isaiah 45:9

When we put ourselves down, bemoaning our looks, our flaws, our perceived lack of ability, we are as that clay vessel that criticizes its maker. And just as ridiculous as it would be for a clay vase to complain to the potter about how it was made, it is also ridiculous for us to complain to the Lord who formed us.

In the eyes of the world, we may be insignificant. We may even appear to some to be worthless. The devil certainly doesn't put much value on us. But, with God, it's a different story. To Him, we are precious. To Him, we are significant. To Him, we are of great value.

Have you ever felt like an ant — tiny, unimportant, too small to really matter? Many people do. We hear them say things like, "I would volunteer my time, but what good could I possibly do?" "I know I could never really make a difference." Or perhaps you have felt like a coney (rock rabbit), shy and ready to run at the slightest sign of difficulty. Yes, we are mere humans, and we can feel like ants or conies at times, but God calls these creatures *"exceeding wise."*

All of these four animals — the ant, the coney, the locust and the spider — have their weaknesses. One locust alone can make very little impact; he must be in a large company to impact his world. And spiders are fragile and easy to kill. Each of these creatures is weak, but each seems to be too busy with his life to really notice his weakness.

Have you ever heard an ant say, "Oh, I'm too stressed to go out to look for food today. I think I'll just sit at home"? Or do spiders consider themselves too fragile to trap insects? I have never seen a rabbit so concerned about his physique that he constantly goes to the gym, working out so that he can show off his muscles. I have never seen a locust constantly exercising, jogging along the road to impress everyone. These creatures are not strong, but neither are they consumed by their weakness.

The first step to success and happiness in God is to recognize and accept your limitations and weaknesses. Until you do, you'll never be happy. So many people try to hide their limitations, pretending to be strong when everything within is crumbling to pieces. Face the truth. As long as you pretend you are strong, you will never seek help outside yourself. How often we wait until it's too late, wanting to cry out for help only when our breath is all but gone. Difficult as it may be, we need to recognize our own weakness.

These four animals *are* weak, but they are also wise. How is that? They recognize their limitations. For instance, ants may carry off the crumbs, but you never see them trying to haul off the entire picnic basket.

When we recognize our limitations, we are free to look to God, the Limitless One. He has no limitation whatsoever. When you place your life in the hands of the unlimited God, you become unlimited as well. Why? Because the unlimited Lord dwells within you. And He is able to become your strength. His grace is sufficient for you, and He is *"able to do exceeding abundantly above all that you could ask or think."*

The apostle Paul declared to the church at Corinth:

And he said unto me, My grace is sufficient for thee: for my strength is made perfect in weakness. Most gladly therefore will I rather glory in my infirmities, that the power of Christ may rest upon me. 2 Corinthians 12:9

What better reason to admit our weakness than to become vessels that show forth His strength? We need to be people who take God at His Word. If He says we are weak, He is right. If He says His power will rest upon us in our weakness, then rest assured that it will.

As you believe God, receive His Word and begin to walk out what He shows you, you begin to move from the realm of the physical into the realm of the supernatural. You move from the realm of the carnal into the realm of the Spirit. You move out of yourself and into Him.

When you admit your weaknesses and trust in Him who is your Strength, you will see things differently. No longer will you look at situations in light of the natural. Instead, you will see with the eyes of the Spirit. You will see yourself as victorious, not defeated; as rich, not poor; as blessed, not cursed; as happy, not despairing.

When we live lives that pretend that we are strong in and of ourselves, and that we have no need of help, then we are contradicting the Scriptures, which declare mankind to be weak. When we live a lie while knowing the truth, we are hypocrites. And hypocrisy is not acceptable to God. This type of hypocrisy proved to be Samson's downfall.

Samson was a Nazarite from birth, destined to be a deliverer of Israel. The signs of his vow were that his hair had never been cut, and he drank no wine. He used his legendary God-given physical strength in fighting against the Philistines, Israel's enemy. Unfortunately, while he was quite strong physically, he didn't have a corresponding strength of character.

Samson was victorious over the Philistines several times, but he loved a Philistine woman. Delilah asked him again and again to reveal to her the source of his great strength. And, as time went on, he gradually weakened in his resolve not to tell her his secret. In his eyes, he was growing stronger and stronger in his own strength. Finally, having told Delilah of his Nazarite vow, Samson seems to have been relying solely upon his own strength rather than upon the Spirit of the Lord:

> *And she said, The Philistines be upon thee, Samson. And he awoke out of his sleep, and said, I will go out as at other times before, and shake myself. And he wist not that the LORD was departed from him.* Judges 16:20

All the *"other times before,"* Samson had deceived Delilah. She had done the things that he had said would cut off his strength, but nothing happened. This time he had told her the truth. She cut his hair while he was sleeping, and now *"the Lord was departed."* Samson's own strength could not save him. His previous exploits, the power he had wielded and the unction under which he had moved could not save him now. Samson had to learn that without the Lord he was nothing.

Have you been relying on things the Lord spoke to you long ago? Perhaps you have been trying to draw your strength from the same experiences, the same songs, the same prophetic words that once brought life and power. But maybe now it just doesn't seem to be working. There is a reason: past victories can encourage us to fight today's battles, but we cannot trust in past victories to get us through today. We cannot look to past glory, or to past visitations of the Lord in our lives. If we do, we start to believe that we are strong in ourselves. That mistake cost Samson his sight and his freedom, and eventually it cost him his life.

Fortunately, the account of Samson doesn't end with Delilah's betrayal. He was not doomed to futile insignificance, a prisoner cast aside and forgotten in some dungeon. He did spend some time in prison, but as he sat there, thinking back over his life, something began to change within him.

As Samson looked to his past victories, to the twenty years he had spent judging Israel, he began to recognize that God had done it all. He repented for having failed God, and his faith began to grow again. He began to feel that God wasn't finished with him yet. He grasped a new sense of destiny. We don't know exactly what he was thinking about in that prison, but it is clear that as his hair began to grow again, so did his faith and strength.

When Samson was called one day to entertain the Philistines at a party, he asked the boy who had charge over him to allow him to lean against the pillars of the house. And God used him again:

And Samson called unto the LORD, and said, O Lord GOD, remember me, I pray thee, and strengthen me, I pray thee, only this once, O God, that I may be at once avenged of the Philistines for my two eyes. And Samson took hold of the two middle pillars upon which the house stood, and on which it was borne up, of the one with his right hand, and of the other with his left. And Samson said, Let me die with the Philistines. And he bowed himself with all his might; and the house fell upon the lords, and upon all the people that were therein. So the dead which he slew at his death were more than they which he slew in his life.

Judges 16:28-30

Samson had finally understood that his strength was not his own. He realized that he had to call upon his God, so that the Lord could show Himself strong in his weakness. Samson had finally become as wise as an ant.

Repentance is a wise course. Don't allow your failures and weaknesses to keep you from returning to God and receiving His grace. When you turn to Him, you will find Him with open arms eagerly awaiting you.

Don't be afraid to recognize and admit your weakness. When you do, the strength of God can be perfected in you. You will never learn to draw strength from God unless you recognize that you need His help. You'll not reach out to God until you realize that you are desperately in need of His assistance. The ant may be a feeble and weak creature, but he has some things to teach all of us.

We too can learn wisdom:

> *The fear of the LORD is the beginning of knowledge: but fools despise wisdom and instruction.*
>
> Proverbs 1:7

"The fear of the LORD"... We hear this term frequently, but what does it mean? It is the understanding that God cannot be contained or controlled. It is the knowledge that He can be dangerous. It is the realization that He alone holds all things, all circumstances and situations, in His hands. And it is the dawning comprehension of the fact that man is not nearly as great as he tries to believe he is. God is all, and we are nothing. It is only by His mercy and grace that we survive.

Part of wisdom lies in beginning to understand our own limitations as well as our capabilities. We need to be as the small creatures of Proverbs 30, who strive to do what they can, but who also know their limits. We are to trust in the Lord, not in our own ability:

> *Thus saith the LORD, Let not the wise man glory in his wisdom, neither let the mighty man glory in his might, let not the rich man glory in his riches: but let him that glorieth glory in this, that*

Small, but Wise

he understandeth and knoweth me, that I am the
LORD which exercise lovingkindness, judgment,
and righteousness, in the earth: for in these things
I delight, saith the LORD.   Jeremiah 9:23-24

Let us be those who *"glory in the LORD."* Let us glory in knowing Him! Our lives are to be lived under His direction. He is the Chief Musician, and only He can direct our lives perfectly. He can draw the music from each of us in such a way as to blend and harmonize with others to bring praise and glory to His Name. Then our lives can exalt the Lord.

But we must be honest with ourselves. We cannot play the trumpet part if we are flutes; we cannot always play the melody, for sometimes we must play the harmony. We must each learn to know what our part is, and we must master that part, for the Lord may call upon us to play at any moment, and we want to be ready for Him.

So let us become wise. Let us acknowledge our limitations as well as our abilities and learn to rely on the Lord. Allow yourself to admit your weakness, so that you can look to God to be your Provider and your Strength.

2

SEARCHING FOR SIGNIFICANCE

Being confident of this very thing, that he which hath begun a good work in you will perform it until the day of Jesus Christ.   Philippians 1:6

We have been created by a loving God, a God who cares for each of us and who has planted within us a destiny and a purpose. He has called each one of us to further His Kingdom, and He is preparing us and gifting us to accomplish specific tasks to that end. Each of us is important, and each contributes as God directs toward the goal of accomplishing His purpose on the earth. I didn't always understand these truths, and I have not always been able to lay hold of them for my own life.

While I was growing up, I was very quiet and shy

— a fact which surprises those who know me now. I had no sense of self-worth, and I didn't think my words or my opinions mattered very much to anyone, so I kept them to myself. Still, I savored in my heart the dream of serving the Lord.

I attended Bible school in the Philippines. While most of the students were high school graduates and many had at least some college training, my level of attainment was about ninth grade on the American scale. I was the shortest, skinniest student in the class and was an introvert who always sat alone at the back of the room.

During class discussions, I hid myself because I was terrified at the thought of having to speak before the other students. I never even prayed out loud in front of them.

My classmates did their homework so beautifully and spoke so eloquently that I ended up feeling like a speck of dust among them. I was nothing! I felt I had nothing to say, nothing to give. As I watched the other students develop, I became very discouraged. Satan tormented me with the thought that I was wasting my time, that I would never be able to stand and preach the Gospel. I was the way I was, and I would surely never change.

The devil said to me, "You might as well go home, back to the province you came from. You might as well quit. You'll never make it! You could never stand in front of a crowd and preach."

At the time, I didn't realize I was listening to the lies of the enemy. It seemed like simple common sense. As I listened, the devil convinced me that I was worthless. Still, in my heart I knew that I was called and chosen by God. I knew that God was bigger than I was and that His resources were unlimited for me. I knew that the Lord had a purpose for my being there. So I struggled on, hoping that something would change.

The teachers at the school also felt that I would never accomplish much, that I would never be anything or anybody in the Kingdom of God, and this created a problem. Because I could not fully pay my tuition, it was subsidized by the school. As wise stewards, it was only right for the school's administrators to think about whether I should be attending the school or not. After all, there were others who were being denied the privilege by my presence. Why should the school continue to underwrite my expenses if I was not going to be able to reap any benefit from it?

Eventually, a faculty meeting was called to decide my fate. The consensus seemed to be that I should go home.

That was exactly what the devil wanted. He wants us to give up and go home and forget any dream we may have of doing anything for Him. He'll even pay our ticket, anything to get us out of the place where we can begin to understand and perform the will of the Lord in our lives.

While the teachers all discussed openly why it was best for me to return home, I felt so discouraged! At one point, I was almost ready to go and start packing before they finished their meeting. Thank God I didn't, because as the meeting neared midnight, one teacher spoke up on my behalf. She wasn't ready to send me back yet, and she felt that God had something planned for my life. "Who are we," she asked, "to determine what God can accomplish with a life?"

That woman was right! Who are you, who am I, to know what God will do in the life of another? Only God can determine how to carry out His own good pleasure and His will in your life. Nothing can hinder the purpose of God in your life — except you. But if you give yourself to God, surrendering your life to Him and allowing Him to move and to work in your life, then you can be what God wants you to be. As you allow God to be what He desires to be in you, He will enable you to be what you want to be. We have the promise:

> *Greater is He that is in you, than he that is in the world.*   1 John 4:4

Only God knows a person's true potential, and He can do "*exceeding abundantly above all that we ask or think*":

Now unto him that is able to do exceeding abun-
dantly above all that we ask or think, according
to the power that worketh in us...

Ephesians 3:20

I was almost sent home from Bible school, but I
wasn't, thanks to the wisdom of that teacher who
spoke up for me. After the meeting that night, I went
to my room, looked in the mirror and said, "These
teachers are right. I am really nothing." But deep
down in my heart, I still knew that I was called by
God, that He had a plan and a purpose for my life. I
knew there was a destiny for me in Him.

And so I prayed, "Lord, I'm not going to go home.
The only place that I will go home to is Heaven. It's
not yet time for me to go there, so I'm staying, Lord,
whatever it takes." Suddenly, God filled me with His
Holy Spirit, and I began to speak in tongues as the
Spirit gave me utterance! As the Spirit of the Lord
baptized me, He loosened my tongue, and from that
day on I began to speak publicly.

In the following days and weeks, the Lord gave
me more courage. I began to face people in confidence. I began to do what I heard God telling me to
do. I began to stand up and speak in class. My sen-
tences were short, but I said what I heard God saying. Everyone was so surprised! Instead of sitting
in the back, I began to sit at the front of the class. I
determined to be what God wanted me to be, and I

purposed in my heart to accomplish the plan of God in my life.

How did all of this happen so suddenly? When God touched me and filled me with His Holy Spirit, He turned my life around so that I could begin to see myself as He sees me. For the first time, I saw myself as being important to God. After all, if I was not important to God, He would not have created me. I began to throw off the attitude of defeat and worthlessness and to allow God to make me what He wanted me to be.

I determined to allow God to work in my life and to develop me as I should be developed. I decided not to withhold anything, but to allow God to do what He decided to do. I grew willing to become what He wanted me to be.

In other words, I corrected my attitude. And what did God do? He prepared and developed me to be a pastor among His people. Nobody could keep me silent anymore, and nothing frightened me. I knew I was a child of God, and so I knew I was important to Him.

No one is insignificant in God's sight. No one is unimportant to Him. You have a place in God's economy. You are part of His program and part of His eternal will.

The devil lied to me and told me I was worthless, a failure, but the grace of God is more than sufficient for us. The power of God is greater than any power of the enemy. Satan is a liar and the father of lies, and his words to me were lies. For I, who could not utter a single word in class, have stood in front of one hundred and seventy thousand people, interpreting for the great evangelist Reinhard Bonnke.

His Word is true:

I can do all things through Christ which strengthen-eth me. Philippians 4:13

What was it that had held me back? It was fear: fear of failure, fear of ridicule, fear of not being as good as the other students. It was a lack of confidence — in God and in myself.

FEAR! LACK! What terrible words! Lack of education! Lack of money! Lack of opportunity! Lack of ability! Lack of strength! These are phrases that we use to describe modern tragedies. But none of these lacks need be a hindrance to those of us who know our God. We don't need all those things to accomplish something great. We just need God.

Do you suffer a lack in some area? Then you are in good company, for all of us are lacking in one way or another. Some of our lacks are real, while others are simply the lies of the enemy. He is trying to discourage us. He wants us to dwell on our lack, focusing on whatever it is that we do not have. He wants these things to be magnified in our souls, so that we come to believe that we cannot serve God because of that one thing we still lack. He wants us to become discouraged. He wants us to feel that we are worthless. His goal is for us to lose the sense of purpose God has for each one of us.

This is a common strategy our enemy uses. If you feel worthless, you won't protect your life and your future. If you feel worthless, you will never step into God's plan for your life. You won't prepare yourself to serve or to minister to others. There would be no point to it. If you have no sense of what God wants to do in your life, you will be satisfied to live with little. You will say, "I was born like this, and I will die like this. There is no reason for me to try to do anything in the Kingdom of God." What a pitiful life that would be!

Stop listening to the lies of the enemy! Make up your mind to have more of God. Begin to see yourself as God sees you. Rise up and become all that God intends you to be. Start conducting yourself the way God expects you to. You are a child of God. Begin to behave that way, speak that way, live that way, think that way. In God's eyes, you are important. You can make a mark on your generation. You can affect the lives of others for the Kingdom.

We must learn to live fully for the Lord. Ask God to show you any area of your life in which He is not enthroned as Lord. As He brings to mind anything which is not pleasing to Him, turn those things around so that you can make something meaningful and beautiful of your life. A life that is fully submitted to God, fully lived out in God, is a life that has purpose and fulfillment.

Don't be surprised if those around you seem to oppose you when you begin to seek the purpose and meaning of your life. Satan tries to come against those who are beginning to discover their destiny in God, and he usually does this through other people. Your friends may think they have your best interests at heart. Your family may think they are only trying to protect you from bring hurt. But when they come to discourage you, it's time to look only to God. Set your face toward Him, tune your heart to hear His voice and press on toward His presence.

As Paul said to the Philippian believers:

> *Brethren, I count not myself to have apprehended: but this one thing I do, forgetting those things which are behind, and reaching forth unto those things which are before, I press toward the mark for the prize of the high calling of God in Christ Jesus. Let us therefore, as many as be perfect, be thus minded: and if in any thing ye be otherwise minded, God shall reveal even this unto you.*
>
> Philippians 3:13-15

"Press" on toward *"the prize,"* which is *"the high calling of God"* in your life!

When we begin to fulfill our destiny in the Lord, others will notice. They won't be able to help it! They will see us living full lives as we do the work God has given us to do and they will want what we have in God, looking to their own calling in Him. This is part of how we can "*stir up one another to good works*" (see Hebrews 10:24).

I have not yet fulfilled all of my destiny in God, but I know that I am fulfilling my calling day by day as I am faithful to do those things that God is giving me to do. The Lord has borne fruit in my life far beyond what I or anyone else could have foreseen during those difficult first days of Bible school, before the Spirit of the Lord laid hold of me. He has brought me a long way since then. I had an experience that reminded me of just how far I have come.

In 1978, I was conducting a family enrichment seminar in Honolulu, Hawaii. One of my former Bible school teachers, a godly woman, attended that meeting. We hadn't seen each other in almost twenty years. She sat at the very front of the room, and she cried all the way through the teaching.

After the seminar was over, she came and threw her arms around me. Still crying, she said, "Ray, please would you forgive me? I want to apologize to you. I'm so sorry."

I said, "Ma'am, why should you apologize to me?"

She took two steps backward, and then answered, "Years ago, when you were at our Bible school, a conference was held concerning your status as a stu-

dent there. I was the one who called for that conference. I was the one who told the others, 'We might
as well send this boy home, for he will never amount
to anything.' As far as I was concerned, you were
wasting my time.

"How wrong I was! Here you are, doing the things
of God that I thought you would never be able to
do. While you were teaching tonight, all I could think
of was, 'This is the handiwork of God.' "

She went on to speak of other students, those who
were more talented or gifted than I had been. She
spoke of those who had graduated with me, whom
everyone believed would make a mark on this world
for the Gospel of Christ Jesus. She told me that one
had left his wife and was no longer serving God.
Another had fallen away to look after the interests
of the world. Several of those we all had thought
would be great in the Kingdom of God were no
longer even serving the Lord.

"In fact," she concluded, "of the twenty-two students in your graduating class, only ten or twelve
are in full-time ministry. And you are the only one
who has traveled around the world to preach the
Gospel. The one we thought would never amount
to anything has shown us all what God can do."

I am not sharing this story to boast of anything I
have done, but I do boast of my God! It is He who
can turn a life around so that what was once seen as
nothing becomes significant and useful to the King-

dom of God. It is He who can turn a heart around so that what was once seen as nothing becomes a heart full to overflowing with the love and life of God. There are no boundaries to what God can do. We are wrong when we place limits upon any person and what He can or will do with his or her life.

You may be thinking, "He could never use me in that way. I know what I heard God telling me to do, but I'm just not gifted in that area. I know God wants to heal me of that hurt, but I guess He can't. I'll have to carry this pain with me forever." This is how man thinks, but it is not how God thinks. What does His Word say?

> *And Jesus looking upon them saith, With men it is impossible, but not with God: for with God all things are possible.*   Mark 10:27

There is no impossibility when you put your trust and confidence in God. Another favorite scripture passage confirms this:

> *I can do all things through Christ which strengtheneth me.*   Philippians 4:13

A more literal translation of this verse might be: "I can do everything God asks of me through the power of Christ which is resident within me." He will not ask us to do anything without equipping us to perform it. Whatever God has planned for you, whatever your purpose, your ministry, your calling in God, you are able to fulfill it in the power of the Christ who lives in you.

You are important to God. You are precious to Him. He has created you with a purpose and a plan in mind. God wants to fulfill His design and His dream for you. If you will surrender your life into the hands of God, He will form you into the person He created you to be, that you can declare the glory of the Lord wherever you go.

God doesn't just have a plan for your own life; He has a plan for the lives of your children and of your spouse. He has a purpose for your marriage and for your home. He has a reason for your situation, your job, your education. No matter who you are, God's plan for you is that you bring glory and honor to His Name. His purpose for you is to know and experience His great love, and that others may come to know His love as He reaches out to them through you.

God is moving among His people. He is stirring individuals, stirring families, stirring churches and stirring nations. Can you sense Him at work in your life?

None of us is insignificant to God. He desires that each one of us respond to Him, no matter how small we feel ourselves to be. As you say "yes" to Him, He will begin to use you. You will begin to blossom in God. You will become a blessing to others, coming out of yourself to proclaim the name of the Lord. Some who are timid will be turned around by God and will not be able to stop speaking about the Lord. Some who have been hiding behind the cloak of religion, or self, or fear, will begin to come out of hiding and to proclaim the name of the Lord.

God wants to change hearts. He wants to place new attitudes within His people. Let Him change you. Let Him change your thoughts, your direction, your assumptions about the way to walk in God. He is saying, "Just put your life in My hand, My child. Surrender to Me, and Me alone. Give over all the things you have been holding back from Me. Trust in Me, and trust in My plans for you. Then you will see what I can do through you."

PART TWO:

THE ANT

3

PRESSING TOWARD THE GOAL

I press toward the mark for the prize of the high calling of God in Christ Jesus.

Philippians 3:14

"What does this Scripture have to do with ants?" you might ask. Quite a lot, actually!

Ants fascinate me. I have watched them at work, and I have learned from them. One thing I have seen is that an ant is consumed with the task before him. If there is a crumb of food left lying somewhere, he will find it. Then he will do whatever is needed to take it back home.

I have sometimes placed crumbs in precarious places to see if ants would go after them. And I was amazed to see what happened. The ants were not afraid of high places. They had no fear for their own safety. They had a total disregard for their own comfort as they labored to carry away the bounty.

It is difficult to stop an ant. Once he has a goal in mind, he will work toward it, no matter what barrier is placed in his way. He may be small, but he is determined. He will overcome every obstacle or difficulty that is placed before him. If you put something in his way, he will simply go over it, under it or around it, keeping his mind set on the goal before him. He will keep pressing forward, regardless of obstacles, until he reaches his goal.

I have even noticed that if one ant is wounded or dying, his companions will not let this stop them from moving toward their goal. They don't sit down and give way to despair. They don't become fearful and discouraged and stop what they are doing.

I have never heard an ant saying, "Alas! My brother has fallen! We will have to give up the pursuit of our goal. It must not be the right thing for us to do right now. God must not want us to gather that crumb!" No, despite the fact that one of their own is wounded, perhaps even mortally so, ants keep moving forward with determination. Nothing seems to stop them.

And nothing seems to make ants afraid, so that they turn away. Once they have focused on a particular goal, they are determined to complete their work.

Pressing Toward the Goal

Humans are another story. People are so afraid to fail! Most people are afraid to even try anything new for fear they might fail. When they encounter problems, they become easily discouraged. When circumstances are not all they could wish, many people turn back from pressing toward their goal. When they see others fall, it has a devastating effect upon them. People are full of fear, but ants are not.

Ants are focused. If there is something they want, ants will try every means to get to it.

Ants encounter difficulties all the time. Yet they just keep marching forward.

If believers come across one small difficulty, we hear them say, "Well, God must be closing the door. This must not be His will for me." But perhaps God is simply testing our determination. Perhaps He is looking to see whether we are truly focused on doing the work He has given to us. We must not be so quick to lay aside the things He places in our hands to do just because some trouble arises.

We need to know what it is that God has called us to do. After all, it is no use our pressing on if we are not pressing on toward some goal. We can accomplish many things, but if they are not the things God has for us, what good are they?

Learn to look to the Lord for His plans for you. Listen to His voice as He whispers His secrets for you into your heart. What is your place in the Kingdom? What is God's plan for you? Why has He birthed you into His family? And why has He redeemed you?

If you are among those who say, "I don't know God's plan for me," or if you feel there is more for you than you are experiencing, you can ask the Lord to show you these things. His Word promises:

> *If any of you lack wisdom, let him ask of God, that giveth to all men liberally, and upbraideth not; and it shall be given him.* James 1:5

God will show you what it is that He has for you to do. He is loving and just. How could He expect you to accomplish His will for you if He refused to show you what that will is?

One problem is that even when we know what it is that we are to do, we often are lazy. It takes energy to minister to others. It takes patience. It takes the ability to rely on the wisdom of God. Unfortunately, none of these things come naturally to us. Most of us would rather sit back and watch someone else do the work. That's why in many churches the pastor is expected to do all of the ministry!

But those who will do the things God gives them to do will be blessed in their obedience. Isn't introducing someone to Christ worth the effort of befriending him in the first place? Isn't the joy of seeing a broken heart mended worth the hours of prayer and counsel required? Isn't watching a young man taking his place in the Kingdom of God worth all the endless trouble it takes to properly raise our children in God?

Unfortunately, people must often be prodded and pushed into doing significant things with their lives. Too often we seek for peace, for rest or for a relaxed rhythm to our lives rather than working toward a worthy goal. While such times can be refreshing, they are not God's whole purpose for us, and He will push us to change. He will arrange our circumstances so that we must change. He will allow us times of refreshing in His presence, but He will also goad us to action when necessary. He is a Shepherd who is not afraid to use His rod to guide us into right paths.

Sometimes the Lord allows us to be stirred to anger at our situations. People often have to grow angry before they will put forth the necessary effort to change their lives. Has Satan been robbing you of the blessing God has for you? Are you tired of putting up with difficult circumstances? Are you "fed up" with fighting for even the smallest victory? Then perhaps it is time to get angry. Perhaps it is time to break out of the mold of your life and press on into greater victory.

Have you ever noticed that people's lives often seem to lack focus? Even the lives of believers are often so cluttered with side issues that they seem to muddle through life. The writer of the book of Hebrews challenges us:

Looking unto Jesus the author and finisher of our faith, who for the joy that was set before him endured the cross, despising the shame, and is set down at the right hand of the throne of God.

Hebrews 12:2

Yet for all our familiarity with this scripture, how focused are our lives? Have we renewed our minds and purified our thoughts, laying aside those things which would distract us from *"looking unto Jesus,"* from fixing our eyes on Him? Fixing our eyes on Jesus will enable us to discover our purpose.

After we focus upon our Lord, then we are also to live our lives in such a way as to clearly show His life flowing in us and through us. And that will happen as we walk out His plan for us and for our families. As we use the gifts, abilities, talents and ministries He has given us, His life in us will be clear for all to see. And it will only happen as our focus is on the Giver of all good things.

In addition to being focused on our goal, as the ant, we must also be careful to carry through with the things we are to accomplish. We should not keep the same goals year after year and never attain them. The book of Proverbs speaks to this when it mentions the ant in another passage:

Go to the ant, thou sluggard; consider her ways, and be wise: which having no guide, overseer, or ruler, provideth her meat in the summer, and gathereth her food in the harvest.

Proverbs 6:6-8

Here the ant is contrasted with the *"sluggard,"* a person who is habitually lazy. The *"sluggard"* is instructed to *"consider"* and learn from the ant. Why? Because ants are industrious, busy and constantly working. You will not find an ant sitting on a rocking chair, trying to pass the time of day. You never find ants that sleep all day. You won't see an ant roaming around the city with no purpose, no direction and no meaning. From sunrise to sunset, the ant is constantly busy seeking food. He is continually enlarging his storehouse, so that he can store more food for the days ahead.

Many people are lazy. They want others to do everything for them. Even in churches there are those who say, "Pray for me, fast for me, worship for me." Why? Usually it is so that the person can rest and do as he pleases.

When you become a Christian, there should be an alteration of your lifestyle. You have passed *"from death unto life"*:

Verily, verily, I say unto you, He that heareth my word, and believeth on him that sent me, hath everlasting life, and shall not come into condemnation; but is passed from death unto life.

John 5:24

As you passed *"from death"* to *"life,"* you were made a new creation. You became part of a new species of being that never existed before:

> *Therefore if any man be in Christ, he is a new creature: old things are passed away; behold, all things are become new.*   2 Corinthians 5:17

"All things" in your life have been transformed; as the Word confirms, *"all things [have] become new."* You should not be today what you were when you were a sinner. There should be an improvement in your life, both in the realm of the physical and in the realm of the spirit.

Have you changed? Are you pressing on into Christ? Are you looking for what He has for you to do and to be? Or are you content to sit back and enjoy what life has to offer you now, thinking that there is no more to it?

Lazy people, sluggards, are those who have no vision. They have no goal in life. They procrastinate, putting everything off until a better time. In Proverbs, just after the sluggard is instructed to *"go to the ant,"* we find this description of that lazy one:

> *How long wilt thou sleep, O sluggard? when wilt thou arise out of thy sleep? Yet a little sleep, a little slumber, a little folding of the hands to sleep:*

Pressing Toward the Goal

So shall thy poverty come as one that travelleth, and thy want as an armed man.

Proverbs 6:9-11

The people of God cannot be lazy people! The army of the Lord is not made up of those who would put everything off until a better time. The company of the victorious in God does not include those who would sleep continually.

Don't wait until tomorrow to do what you should be doing today. What you are today will determine what you will be tomorrow. Your eternity depends on what you are and what you do *today*.

Don't wait until later to mean business with God. "Later" might never come. So don't wait until you retire to make peace with God. Don't wait until you finish college to give your life to the Lord. Don't wait until you build up your career to work at building His Kingdom. As one who is wise, take every opportunity to proclaim the Lord, whether by your words or your actions.

Lazy people will never progress. They will never advance, whether in the natural (in their jobs) or in the spiritual (in the Kingdom of God).

People who are busy and active are less likely to get sick, but those who are lazy and get no exercise will die young. The life of the one who is always active will be prolonged, and he will be happier, more joyful. So let's not waste our time, but place our focus on God and on fulfilling our destiny in Him.

For a time, I served as Director of our Christian school in the Philippines and it fell to me to discipline any erring teachers. One man was always late. At the beginning of the school year, he was usually about five minutes late every morning. After the first two or three weeks, however, he started arriving ten minutes late. Then it was half an hour or forty-five minutes. How could he properly do his job with so little time to teach the class? And what kind of example was he for the students? I said, "This cannot continue," so I called him into my office.

I came right to the point with him. "Why are you always late?" I asked.

"Pastor, it's too hard to get up in the morning," he answered.

What a dumb answer! I thought, as though it was easy for everyone else to get up and be on time. I told the man that this was no excuse, and that if he wanted to continue teaching, he had to come on time.

"Well, today is payday," I told him. "Let's go to a store, so you can buy an alarm clock." I took him personally to buy the clock.

I was very distressed, therefore, when the man continued to arrive late. I would have to substitute for him. I began to think, "Why should I be wasting my time working for this man when he's paid to be here? Why should I do his work?" So I called him to my office again. "I have given you notice about being late, " I told him. " I had to teach your class for you on a number of occasions. I'm sorry, but your services will no longer be required at this school."

With this, the teacher began to cry. When I saw the tears, my heart melted. I said to him, "I believe I have extended grace to you already, and enough is enough. But, you may stay. From now on, however, every minute that you are late I will deduct from your salary." And do you know what? That solved the problem. From that time on, the man was never late.

People who are lazy are not serious about what they are doing. They do things when they feel like it.

Sometimes we consider the things of God to be common and ordinary. We think, "This is just temporary." But we need to realize that everything that is involved in our spiritual lives is for eternity. And even something as simple as showing up for work on time is part of our spiritual lives.

It didn't matter whether that teacher was the best mathematician in the world. If he was lazy, I couldn't use him. You might have all the talent in the world. You might have great ability. You might have all the qualities of being a good leader. But if you're lazy, all of your gifts mean nothing.

The Scriptures teach us diligence, diligence of spirit and of behavior:

Keep thy heart with all diligence; for out of it are the issues of life.   Proverbs 4:23

One of the major reasons we fail is that we are careless. We are not diligent in using the things that God has given us. That is why we miss out on some of the blessings of the Lord.

The Word of God tells us:

Work out your own salvation with fear and trembling.   Philippians 2:12

Our relationship with Jesus Christ is a serious matter, and being lazy is no excuse. Let us be wise and diligent like the ant, entering into the Kingdom of God with all our hearts and striving to possess everything that God has for us.

4

PREPARING FOR ANY EVENTUALITY

The ants are a people not strong, yet they prepare their meat in the summer. Proverbs 30:25

The ant, as we have seen, is diligent. Always busy, these tiny creatures refuse to be distracted from their goals. They are not lazy, but are continually working, striving even when those around them fall.

But the ant is not busy just for the sake of activity. He has not bought into society's vision of activity as a means of proving one's importance or worth. No, the ant has a specific purpose. Although he is not strong, he is constantly preparing for the days to come. Have you ever found an ant sleeping? Have you ever come across one sitting in a corner weeping because of discouragement?

Part of what we are to learn from the wisdom of the ant, I believe, is that we are to be ready for whatever life brings. We are to be busy preparing ourselves so that we are able to be used of the Lord whenever He wants us. This is a lesson some find difficult.

While I was working as a missionary in Guam, I learned that the islands were susceptible to hurricanes. So many strong storms would sweep in from the ocean over that island that certain buildings were designated as public shelters. When the alarm sounded, you needed to stop whatever you were doing and go to the nearest shelter. Some people, as it turned out, were too preoccupied or too lazy to respond to that warning, and many of them lost their lives as a result.

That alarm signaled danger. It meant that an enemy was approaching, one that could destroy your life if you failed to take shelter fast enough. How could anyone ignore such a call? Yet some did.

Sometimes we hear alarms sounding in our lives. We should be alarmed when we find that we are no longer praying or reading the Word as we should. We should be alarmed if we find that sin is overtaking us. Sometimes we sense that the enemy is on the attack. This is cause for alarm.

Yet we should not wait until we hear an alarm to make sure all is well in our lives. We need to be continually preparing, lest life's difficulties overtake us.

We must also be ready so that we may be used of God. And we must be prepared to stand before Him.

The prophet Amos wrote:

Prepare to meet thy God.   Amos 4:12

One day each of us will stand before God to give an account. There is no escape from that day, for every man will be judged. And while we are not yet standing in His Presence, we need to use our time wisely. We must prepare.

I try to be prepared for the everyday things in life. For example, every evening I choose my clothes for the following day. It's a small decision, yet I know that I will have pressing things to do the following day, and I don't want to be delayed by having to stand in front of my closet deciding what to wear. So when I climb into bed at night, I feel relaxed in knowing what I will wear the next morning.

Not everyone has to do that because not everyone lacks the gift of color coordination as I do. I know my inability, however, so I prepare ahead of time. Otherwise, I would quickly put on the first thing I saw in the closet. Then, when I got to wherever I was going, I would discover (or someone else would discover for me) that nothing matched.

I do the same thing with breakfast decisions. I plan at night what I will eat the following morning. I don't want to stand numbly before the refrigerator in the morning wondering what I should eat. I have no time to waste, so I must be ready.

In the same way, when I stand before God, I don't want to wonder if I have done the right thing. I want to be ready in that moment. So I plan, and prepare, and do the things that I know I need to do.

Just as my decisions each night save time and effort the following day, so the decisions we make each day will either help or hinder us in our walk with God. Many of the choices we make in our Christian lives come down to one simple basic decision:

> *And if it seem evil unto you to serve the LORD, choose you this day whom ye will serve; whether the gods which your fathers served that were on the other side of the flood, or the gods of the Amorites, in whose land ye dwell: but as for me and my house, we will serve the LORD.*
>
> Joshua 24:15

We don't know when we will face that day for which we need to be prepared. We must set our lives in order now, before it's too late.

> *In those days was Hezekiah sick unto death. And the prophet Isaiah the son of Amoz came to him, and said unto him, Thus saith the LORD, Set thine house in order; for thou shalt die, and not live.*
>
> 2 Kings 20:1

Preparing for Any Eventuality

What would you do if you knew you were to die tomorrow? If you are like most people, you would probably spend your last moments in the House of God, making certain that everything was settled between you and Him.

The problem is that we don't know when the end is coming. We don't usually know exactly when we will die. And we don't know when Christ is returning. The Bible tells us:

> *For yourselves know perfectly that the day of the Lord so cometh as a thief in the night.*
>
> 1 Thessalonians 5:2

No announcement will be made — beyond what the Word of God has already proclaimed. There will be no warning on the evening news. We don't know when Christ will come. But whenever He comes, don't be found sleeping like the foolish virgins:

> *Then shall the kingdom of heaven be likened unto ten virgins, which took their lamps, and went forth to meet the bridegroom. And five of them were wise, and five were foolish. They that were foolish took their lamps, and took no oil with them: but the wise took oil in their vessels with their lamps. While the bridegroom tarried, they all slumbered and slept. And at midnight there was a cry made, Behold, the bridegroom cometh; go ye out to meet*

him. Then all those virgins arose, and trimmed their lamps. And the foolish said unto the wise, Give us of your oil; for our lamps are gone out. But the wise answered, saying, Not so; lest there be not enough for us and you: but go ye rather to them that sell, and buy for yourselves. And while they went to buy, the bridegroom came; and they that were ready went in with him to the marriage: and the door was shut. Afterward came also the other virgins, saying, Lord, Lord, open to us. But he answered and said, Verily I say unto you, I know you not. Watch therefore, for ye know neither the day nor the hour wherein the Son of man cometh. Matthew 25:1-13

Don't take this risk. Keep your lamp filled with the oil of the Holy Spirit. Be ready; be prepared; be filled up with God:

Wherefore be ye not unwise, but understanding what the will of the Lord is. And be not drunk with wine, wherein is excess; but be filled with the Spirit. Ephesians 5:17-18

A more accurate translation of this verse might be: "Be being filled with the Spirit." In other words, be continually filled and refilled with Him. Don't allow yourself to run out of the Holy Spirit, but allow Him to be filling you over and over. Be prepared.

Preparing for Any Eventuality

Jesus said:

Watch therefore: for ye know not what hour your Lord doth come. But know this, that if the goodman of the house had known in what watch the thief would come, he would have watched, and would not have suffered his house to be broken up. Therefore be ye also ready: for in such an hour as ye think not the Son of man cometh.

Matthew 24:42-44

We are living in a time of opportunity. Now is the time to be productive, to be fruitful for the Lord, to be useful to Him. Yes, it is easier to let others do the work of ministry, but nowhere does the Word say, "Thou shalt take thine ease and cause others to bear all the burden alone." We are to encourage one another, help one another, bless one another. And together we are to journey through this life.

We are each responsible for what the Lord has placed in our hands to do. We are not to sit back and watch others do what God has called us to perform. You may think you have chosen an easier path for now, but one day when your strength is gone, when you realize that your life is coming to an end, you will be filled with grief if you haven't taken every opportunity life has offered you to fulfill your calling and destiny in God.

Yes, God can do His work without us. Yes, He can

find others who will be willing to do His bidding. But do we really want to miss the blessing and the joy of serving Him? We are called to be *"laborers together with God."* He wants us to share in the joy of blessing others. So don't hesitate. Don't go unprepared. Take advantage of your opportunity!

> *And the Lord said, Who then is that faithful and wise steward, whom his lord shall make ruler over his household, to give them their portion of meat in due season? Blessed is that servant, whom his lord when he cometh shall find so doing. Of a truth I say unto you, that he will make him ruler over all that he hath.* Luke 12:42-44

Let us be as the *"faithful and wise steward,"* bringing forth meat to those who need it in the House of the Lord. Be prepared to serve at all times, and in whatever ways the Lord desires.

We are soldiers in the army of the Lord, and we know that a soldier must be prepared, ready to carry out his orders. Whenever a soldier hears the trumpet sound in the morning, he jumps out of bed, ready to do whatever is expected of him that day. His motivation may be that he doesn't want to do any push-ups, or maybe he doesn't want to be assigned to KP duty. Whatever the motivation, however, he moves. He never says, "I think I'll just sleep in for a while." A soldier would rather get up than face the consequences of his laziness. We must be just as motivated in the Kingdom of God.

What are the consequences of laziness? We might not walk as closely with God as we could, or we might even lose the sense of His abiding presence with us.

Our lack of discipline can affect others as well. Who will teach our children? Who will preach the Word? Who will share the Good News? Who will feed the hungry, help the sick, aid the poor? Who will do these things, if not you and I?

Get ready:

> *Let us be glad and rejoice, and give honour to him: for the marriage of the Lamb is come, and his wife hath made herself ready.* Revelation 19:7

Let us make ourselves ready. The Bridegroom could come any day now. The trumpet could sound at any moment. The archangel could shout at any second. Are you ready?

As a pastor, I have had to warn some successful businessmen who only got to church once or twice a month. It is not wrong to be industrious and hard-working, but if we do everything else and fail to prepare ourselves spiritually, what have we gained?

Some people work themselves to death, storing up riches to leave to the Antichrist. I can't tell them not to work, but I can tell them that they should also take time for God.

One family laughingly told me, "Don't worry, pastor. We live close to you. If the trumpet sounds, we'll just take hold of you and go up with you." But others cannot do your preparation. You must do it for yourself.

Evaluate your life and begin to understand what it is that is worth striving for. Grow as wise as the ant, which prepares for what is ahead. Ants may not be strong, but they're wise. They may lack riches, but they're wise. They never starve to death.

When winter comes, ants are not caught off guard. They have worked all summer long, storing up everything they need, so that they can live comfortably through the coldest weather. In the same way, we need to prepare for eternity.

Be prepared for danger:

> *Be sober, be vigilant; because your adversary the devil, as a roaring lion, walketh about, seeking whom he may devour.*   1 Peter 5:8

Be prepared. Be watchful. Be on guard. Because I know that I am weak, I'm always on guard. I try not to take chances, because I know my limitations. Therefore, I need to continually improve myself and continually be on my guard, because my enemy is stronger and more powerful than I am.

He has overpowered me before, so I need to be protected from him. And the only way I can be protected from him is to place my life in the hands of God and be ready to strike when the enemy comes.

Jesus in me is greater than all the forces of the enemy that rise up against me, and Jesus in you is greater than all the forces of the enemy that rise up against you! You can overcome:

> *Ye are of God, little children, and have overcome them: because greater is he that is in you, than he that is in the world.*   1 John 4:4

Praise God, He is "*greater*"! We must reach out to Him with all of our strength, knowing that He is our life.

Be wise like an ant. Be mindful of the things of God. Don't live for today alone. Consider tomorrow, and strive toward the goals God has for you. Provide for your needs — those of the future as well as those of the moment.

We can prepare for the future by being good stewards of what God has given to us. This includes the Word of the Lord and every spiritual gift with which He has supplied us. We must be careful to nurture those things He has placed within our spirits and to grow in our Christian lives.

We must also be good stewards of those things the Lord has provided in the natural. Too often believers tend to either become enslaved by earthly goods or neglect stewardship entirely. But we are to do neither, using our money and our goods wisely without allowing them to become a snare for our souls.

I have never seen a wasteful ant. I have never seen one wasting his time or his energy. I have never seen one rushing to acquire things he does not need — even if it was on sale!

If we are not wise, we will be wasteful. We need to plan how our money will be spent. I have seen too many Christians who are millionaires one day and paupers thirty days later. They spend their paychecks as soon as they get them, and then they have nothing for the rest of the month. Learn to manage your money. Control it; don't let it control you.

Too often, when some people see something they want, they say, "Oh, I don't have the money for it right now, but I believe in the Lord." Then out comes the charge card. I call that "plastic faith." When the bills come in, they are not nearly so happy. They say, "Oh, God, how did this happen?"

I wouldn't go so far as to say that believers should not have credit cards, but if you can't exercise self-control in this area, and if you don't spend wisely, you are bringing yourself into bondage. You are creating a house for a poor man. So be wise. Plan ahead, and don't become enslaved to debt.

Most of our financial problems arise because either we don't value what we do have or we don't plan ahead. Let us be good stewards of God's blessings. If you can only be trusted with fifty dollars, then no matter how much you pray for God to give you a million dollars, He'll never give it to you. There are people who say, "If I only had ten thousand dollars ...," but when they receive something from God, they squander it.

Once a man came to his pastor and said, "Pastor, will you please pray for my business? Please pray that the Lord will prosper it so that I can give to the work of God." So the pastor prayed. The business was blessed, and the owner started giving his tithes. First he gave twenty dollars a week, then fifty, then one hundred.

The man came back to the pastor, saying, "Pastor, God is blessing my business. Would you please pray that God would greatly expand my business so that I can give more?" Again the Lord blessed the business. Eventually, the man was tithing five hundred dollars a week. Then, before long, he was giving two thousand dollars a week.

Suddenly the man seemed to disappear. He was no longer active in the church. The pastor visited him and asked, "What's the matter?"

He said, "Pastor, I'm having a hard time. Now that the business is blessed and prospering, it's too difficult for me to give my tithes. The tithe would now be four thousand dollars a week. Please pray for me. I'm having great difficulty giving that much."

The pastor asked the businessman, "Was five hundred a week too difficult to give?"

He answered, "No, Pastor, that was not too difficult for me to give."

Then the pastor took the hands of the businessman and prayed, "Lord, bless this business to the extent that this brother can tithe five hundred dollars a week." When the man protested, the pastor said, "But I thought that was how much you wanted to be blessed."

And the man responded, "Forget it, Pastor. Here's my tithe."

So this man learned to value the blessing and provision of God more than think of the amount he gave to Him. This is how we are to be. We are to value God and His purposes above anything we have. Focus on the Blesser and not on the blessing. He provided *"the Pearl of Great Price"*:

> *Again, the kingdom of heaven is like unto a merchant man, seeking goodly pearls: who, when he had found one pearl of great price, went and sold all that he had, and bought it.*
>
> Matthew 13:45-46

Be a good steward of what God has given you. Like the ant, be prepared for whatever God brings your way. Be ready in the natural, and in the spiritual, for you don't know when the Lord will require it from your hand. As the Scriptures declare:

> *Preach the word! Be ready in season and out of season. Convince, rebuke, exhort, with all long-suffering and teaching.*
>
> 2 Timothy 4:2, NKJ

PART THREE:

THE CONEY

5

Recognizing Your Weaknesses

The conies are but a feeble folk, yet make they their houses in the rocks.　　　Proverbs 30:26

"Coney" is a term we don't use very often these days. What is a coney? It's a rock rabbit, a type of rabbit that lives among the rocks, usually in desert places.

As the Word of God says, rabbits are "*a feeble folk.*" They are in constant danger from predators and are vulnerable to attack. These animals have no real means of defending themselves. They are not fierce like the lion, or venomous like some snakes. Because they are incapable of defense, they must resort to other means of survival.

The first thing we can see in these creatures is that they are unpretentious. They know their weakness, and there is no hypocrisy in them. They don't try to bluff larger animals. They don't try to fight back against their predators. They know who they are, and they know their limitations. Yet they are determined to survive.

Coneys have no reason to hide their shortcomings. They have to face their weaknesses squarely if they hope to exist alongside stronger animals.

So how do rock rabbits survive? They are very fast runners. And where do they run? They run to the rocks. They know they will be safe there, so that is where they make their homes. The rocks provide a place of safety, for there the coneys will be camouflaged and hidden. Also, to ensure that the species survives despite predators, rock rabbits reproduce abundantly, as do most rabbit species.

Like the coney, we must face our limitations. If we don't learn to trust in the mercy and grace of God, we will be gobbled up by life's predators before we even know what happened.

Many times we try to pretend that everything is all right. We don't want to admit to others that we have problems, that we are hurting inside. We try to cover up how we feel. After all, if we're really following Jesus, everything must be all right. Right?

And so we try to live in our own strength. But if we never admit our weakness, we will never ask for God's strength.

It is not a sin to admit your need. It is not shameful to admit that you need help. It is not wrong to reach out to your brothers and sisters around you. We can help each other. When you are feeling weak, I will give you a hand. And when I am feeling weak, I may need your help too. Don't be ashamed of that.

Don't be afraid to admit your need to God and to ask for His strength, and don't be afraid to admit your need to your brothers and sisters in the Lord, those who are stronger and who have a heart to minister to and strengthen their brethren. Sometimes we need to lean on the strength of another. This is one way the Lord teaches us to have a spirit of humility, for it does away with pride in our lives.

You don't have to laugh when you feel like crying. You don't have to smile when it seems that your world is crumbling. That moment when you are at your weakest is the moment in which you can experience the supernatural strength of the Lord. If you never come to the end of yourself, you will never turn to God. The end of yourself is the beginning of God in you. If you keep on struggling, trying to find a way to overcome on your own, then you will struggle alone. But when you come to such times, cry out, "Lord, help me! I am weak and can't make it on my own." Then the Lord God will be there to lift you up and strengthen you.

The apostle Paul was not afraid to admit his weaknesses. He was also not afraid to commend himself to the strength of the Lord.

And he said unto me, My grace is sufficient for thee: for my strength is made perfect in weakness. Most gladly therefore will I rather glory in my infirmities, that the power of Christ may rest upon me. Therefore I take pleasure in infirmities, in reproaches, in necessities, in persecutions, in distresses for Christ's sake: for when I am weak, then am I strong. 2 Corinthians 12:9-10

Never be ashamed to ask a brother or sister to pray for you. Satan will try to shame you into believing that you don't need the prayers of others. Your own pride will hold you back. But humility and honesty will bring you deliverance through Christ.

If you are in a place in your life where you are stronger in God and you see someone else struggling in life, know that you have no right to criticize that person. You have no right to step on a person who is struggling and to push him down even further. Help those who are struggling. Support them, lift them up. Be one on whom they can lean for strength. In this way, you will be a blessing to the people of God. And God will bless you as you bless and strengthen others.

Recognizing Your Weaknesses

Ministry to those who are weak is part of what the Lord has called us to do:

I have shewed you all things, how that so labour-ing ye ought to support the weak, and to remem-ber the words of the Lord Jesus, how he said, It is more blessed to give than to receive. Acts 20:35

Now we exhort you, brethren, ... comfort the feebleminded, support the weak, be patient toward all men. 1 Thessalonians 5:14

Allow your words to be ones that bring encouragement. Use your actions to strengthen God's people. In this way, we work with the Lord to build up His house.

One day you will be feeling weaker yourself. One day it will be your turn to endure a season of struggle. Then you will need a helping hand to minister life to you. You will need someone to pray with you, to encourage you, to strengthen you in the Word. And then you will see that what you have sown, you will also reap. Others will be glad to bless you, for you will have proven a blessing to their lives.

Do you want to be one who strengthens God's people? Do you want to be one who builds up His Church? Do you want to be the *"restorer of cities in which to dwell,"* the one who *"lifts up the hands which hang down"*? Then allow the Lord to do these things through you. And watch to see the blessing that He brings to His people.

It's not important that we be recognized. We don't need to be considered great in order for God to use us. We don't need to pretend that we are "somebody" in order to be noticed by the Lord. He doesn't think the way men think, and He doesn't see as we see. He doesn't care for the few and neglect the rest:

> *For the LORD seeth not as man seeth; for man looketh on the outward appearance, but the LORD looketh on the heart.* 1 Samuel 16:7

When you were born again into the family and household of God, you became somebody in Him. You are important to God for that reason alone. He created you. He loves you. He could not care for you any more deeply than He does right now. So don't buy into the lie that says we must become spiritual superstars. What we are to become is whatever it is that God has destined for us to be. What we are to do is that which He has given us to do.

Too often we live in the misty land of excuses. There we seek to excuse ourselves for not doing the things that we think we should be doing. Our focus is on our limitations, as we gaze into our own perceived nothingness. But there must be no excuses if we are obeying the Lord to the best of our ability.

We don't need to worry about those things we cannot do, but about those that we can do and that the Lord has asked us to do. The Word of God teaches:

> *For if there is first a willing mind, it is accepted according to what one has, and not according to what he does not have.*
> 2 Corinthians 8:12, NKJ

The gift is "*acceptable*" according to what we have, not what we don't have! Don't excuse yourself any longer. Don't worry about your limitations and about your seeming insignificance. If God has given you a work to do, He Himself will tear down the walls of limitation and enable you to perform the task.

> *But one and the same Spirit works all these things, distributing to each one individually as He wills.*
> 1 Corinthians 12:11, NKJ

There is not a single person alive who does not possess some gifting from God. There is not a single person alive who is totally lacking in talent. The Lord has given gifts to all, distributing them by the Holy Spirit, as He wills. He has measured out certain gifts to be given to all who believe:

> *For I say, through the grace given unto me, to every man that is among you, not to think of him-*

*self more highly than he ought to think; but to
think soberly, according as God hath dealt to every
man the measure of faith.* Romans 12:3

*But unto every one of us is given grace according
to the measure of the gift of Christ.*

Ephesians 4:7

Faith, grace and the life of Christ within have been measured out to each man, but these gifts can grow in our lives. Therefore, there is no acceptable excuse for not being actively involved in the Kingdom of God.

Our Lord has called us for a purpose. He has called us for a reason, to be a people of destiny. We will arrive at our destiny as we allow God to move and operate in our lives, but we must not limit what He can do.

This may be a little difficult for some to understand. After all, we all know that God is great and awesome. We all know that He can do anything He desires. So why would anyone try to limit Him? We may not do so knowingly, but we do limit Him nevertheless. Every time we draw back from the things He has asked of us we are limiting Him. Someone may say, "I don't have the faith to pray for this situation!" "I would love to be a pastor, but I don't know how I could possibly afford the training." "I wish God would send someone to witness to that person.

I'd love to see her come to the Lord, but I can't say anything about it to her. What if she rejects me?"

We limit God by placing Him within the framework of our own limited thinking. It is time to let God out of the box! Let Him flow forth from you unhindered by your own concepts. Seek out His work in your life. Bask in His touch.

As you allow the Lord's work in your life, you will gain strength, but that strength will be God's and not your own. His strength will be perfected in your weakness, but only as you admit that you are weak.

When we are willing to face our weaknesses, we open ourselves to the Lord, to bring forth His strength in us. Those who are weak need someone stronger than themselves. They need someone who is able to come alongside them and protect them or defend them.

The weak should not be looked down on by the strong, and the strong should not be boasting over the weak. The weak should not be intimidated by the strong. Both need each other, for God created the weak to be blessed by the strong, and God created the stronger to uphold and support the weaker. The weak and the strong can minister to one another so that they can be mutually blessed:

We then that are strong ought to bear the infirmities of the weak, and not to please ourselves.

Romans 15:1

For we are glad, when we are weak, and ye are strong: and this also we wish, even your per-fection.   2 Corinthians 13:9

When we are weak, we should graciously receive the ministry of those who are strong in the Lord. But there is also someone else who will help us and will be strong on our behalf.

We can see this at work in the story of two brothers. The younger was being bullied by some older boys at school. They tormented him and baited him. He tried to get away from them, but they continued to bully him, and he could do nothing about it. Finally, he could stand it no longer, so he told his older brother what was happening.

The next day at school the older brother was watching from a little way off when the bigger boys came to bully his brother again. The younger boy called to his brother. Suddenly the bullies were faced with a young man who was larger than they. He looked at them sternly, as if he meant business, and said, "What are you guys doing?" And all of those bullies ran away.

The younger boy had someone larger on his side. He had someone to speak up for him, to fight for him if necessary. He had someone who could challenge his tormentors and win.

Well, we have a big Brother, don't we? His name is Jesus Christ. He is there when we need Him to

fight for us. He will face every enemy on our behalf. And He will always win, for He is greater than
any enemy who could possibly come against us.

*Because the foolishness of God is wiser than men;
and the weakness of God is stronger than men.*
1 Corinthians 1:25

But there is one problem: we will not call for help
if we refuse to recognize that we need it. We will
not seek help if we fail to recognize that we need
somebody to come to our rescue.

I believe that the reason people are not praying
and calling on God, the reason they are not trusting
in Him, is that they are not fully convinced they are
weak. But when a person comes to realize that he is
in trouble, when he sees that he is desperately in
need, then he will do anything he can to get help.

We usually see being weak as a negative thing.
Our society doesn't value humility. Admitting the
need for others or for God is viewed as a sign that a
person is somehow deficient, lacking in independence. But that is not how God sees things.

*But God hath chosen the foolish things of the world
to confound the wise; and God hath chosen the
weak things of the world to confound the things
which are mighty.* 1 Corinthians 1:27

God has chosen "*the weak*." If you are weak, if you feel that you simply cannot make it on your own without the help of the Lord and of His people, then you have been chosen of God to amaze those who believe themselves strong. He said:

Let the weak say, I am strong.   Joel 3:10

Weakness, according to God, is strength. To the natural mind this makes little sense, but we must realize that it is only as we admit our weaknesses that God can show Himself to be powerfully strong on our behalf.

Take a close look at your life and know that you are in a position of weakness. Then understand that God alone is your strength.

There can be no hypocrisy in the Kingdom of God. There can be no pretense. The sooner we realize that we are nothing without our Lord, the more we will cling to Him in surrender and faithfulness. The more fully we realize that our lives are empty without God, the more we will allow Him to have dominion and authority and rulership over us.

Rock rabbits are weak, but they don't try to hide that fact. Unfortunately, many Christians pretend to be strong when in reality they have been defeated by the enemy. You will never have victory over that type of hypocrisy until you realize your true condition. Once you accept the fact of your weakness, you will begin to experience abundant victory. Embrace the humility necessary to face your failings and when you do, the Lord will raise you up:

> *Humble yourselves therefore under the mighty hand of God, that he may exalt you in due time.*
> 1 Peter 5:6

When we are weak, we can experience the power of God and the ability of God, to work in our lives. Our times of weakness are the times in which we can experience the supernatural moving of God in a greater way. When we are strong, we tend to depend on our own strength and ability. Like the coney, we need to know where our true refuge lies.

Like the coney, we must realize our insignificance apart from the Rock. Hidden in the Rock, we regain our true significance. Hiding in the Rock allows us to fulfill our true destiny.

6

TAKING REFUGE IN THE ROCK

God is our refuge and strength, a very present help in trouble. Psalm 46:1

As we have seen, the coney is a weak animal, sought by predators. Since he has no real means of defense, he survives by living among the rocks, where he is difficult to see and to catch.

We are to learn the wisdom of the rock rabbit. We, too, are plagued by an enemy, one who would love to devour us. But, like the coney, we are to know our place of refuge:

The high hills are a refuge for the wild goats; and the rocks for the conies. Psalm 104:18

"The high hills" signify places of pride or self-exaltation in our lives. These are the places of our own human strength apart from God. And this is the abiding place of the wild goat. In the Word of God, goats often signify sin. The Lord instructed Israel through Moses that the priest was to take two goats from the sons of Israel:

> *And Aaron shall cast lots upon the two goats; one lot for the LORD, and the other lot for the scapegoat. And Aaron shall bring the goat upon which the LORD's lot fell, and offer him for a sin offering. But the goat, on which the lot fell to be the scapegoat, shall be presented alive before the LORD, to make an atonement with him, and to let him go for a scapegoat into the wilderness.*
>
> Leviticus 16:8-10

Wild goats are difficult to catch. They cannot easily be trained or domesticated. They are swift and can easily evade capture on the high mountains. Being wild, they go wherever they want, whenever they want.

So it is within each one of us. There are wild goats on the hills of self-exaltation in our lives. These are the sins that seem to be so difficult for us to deal with. They may be attitudes or sins of the mind — capriciously going wherever they want, and very hard to lay hold of and deal with.

Taking Refuge in the Rock

But we are not to be wild goats. Rather, we are to be rock rabbits who live in their place of refuge. We are to cling to the Rock, which is the Lord God. Then we will be difficult for any enemy to catch.

Like the coney, we are to be camouflaged. In other words, we are to be so like our Refuge that when others look at us, what they see is the Rock. We are to be so like Him that we are hidden in Him, camouflaged from view. The psalmist declared:

> *Thou art my hiding place; thou shalt preserve me*
> *from trouble; thou shalt compass me about with*
> *songs of deliverance.*   Psalm 32:7

God is our *"hiding place."* We can run to Him and be hidden. He is our secret place of refuge and safety. As the rabbit runs to his lair, so may we run to God:

> *The name of the LORD is a strong tower: the*
> *righteous runneth into it, and is safe.*
> Proverbs 18:10

God has created the rock rabbit with the ability to be hidden among the rocks. He can blend in and become difficult for a predator to detect. If a rabbit is lying still among the rocks, his enemy will not be able to find him to devour him because he is camouflaged. Even if he is in plain sight, he is hidden from the eyes of his enemy.

But what about us? How do we become camouflaged? How do we become hidden in God? Paul
wrote:

*But put ye on the Lord Jesus Christ, and make
not provision for the flesh, to fulfil the lusts thereof.*
Romans 13:14

"Put[ting] on the Lord Jesus Christ" is like laying
hold of our camouflage. It is our means of being hidden. Our goal is to grow so Christlike that when
others look at us, what they see is Him.

Please don't misunderstand. We don't actually
become little Christs, any more than the coneys become little rocks. If a predator, perhaps a wolf, smells
the scent of a coney, it will know it is there, even if it
cannot see the rabbit. It is not fooled into thinking
that the rabbit has become a rock. But what would
be the use of the wolf attacking a mound of rocks in
hopes of capturing a small rabbit? The rock is hard
and jagged, its sharp edges serving as the rabbit's
defense. No wolf would attack a rock just because
there was a rabbit there.

In the same way, we are to be hidden in God. Our
enemy will know we are there, but he will not try to
attack God Himself in hopes of flushing us out of
our Refuge. He may be hungry, and he may snarl
and rage, but when we are in our Refuge, our *strong
tower,*" he cannot get to us. If we are walking in re-

94

pentance, in purity and uprightness, then the devil will have no place in us.

The devil can be a fierce predator. As Peter wrote, he goes about *"like a lion"*:

> *Be sober, be vigilant; because your adversary the*
> *devil walks about like a roaring lion, seeking whom*
> *he may devour.* 1 Peter 5:8, NKJ

Since we know this, it would be foolish for us to wander far from our place of refuge. It would be senseless for us to allow him to make us his prey. We need to stand against the devil in our weakness. And then something wonderful will happen.

As we face our enemy in our weakness, then the Lord truly becomes our Strength. The enemy, the one who likes to appear as a lion, may think he is pursuing a poor little coney who is scampering among the rocks to find a place of safety. But his laugh of triumph will turn to a scream of fright when the Lion of Judah comes leaping from the rocks in our defense!

Let the Lion of Judah roar from within you. Let Him arise in you and be manifested through you. The Bible tells us that the battle is not ours, but the Lord's. Christ will fight on behalf of His people. We are part of His army. And the members of an army fight their battles together.

As a matter of fact, our Lord has already overcome our enemy and put that devil under His power, dominion and authority. If you are weak, rely on the One who is your Strength. Flee to the Rock, that place of refuge, and don't stay there only when you see the enemy coming. Learn from the coney. Dwell in the Rock; abide in the Lord; live in your place of refuge. Make the Lord God your dwelling place, and you will be safe from your enemy.

Throughout the Scriptures we see this idea of abiding in God. It is as though He was inviting us repeatedly to dwell in Him.

> LORD, *thou hast been our dwelling place in all generations.* Psalm 90:1

> *He that dwelleth in the secret place of the most High shall abide under the shadow of the Almighty.* Psalm 91:1

> *Mine eyes shall be upon the faithful of the land, that they may dwell with me: he that walketh in a perfect way, he shall serve me.* Psalm 101:6

> *Abide in me, and I in you. As the branch cannot bear fruit of itself, except it abide in the vine; no more can ye, except ye abide in me.* John 15:4

Are you weak? Then look to the Word. Over and over God declares Himself to us. He is our Strength, our Victory, our Joy and Confidence. He is our Defense, our Refuge, our Hiding Place. He is our Fortress and our Place of Safety. In Him, we are protected and kept. God is our Source, and all things we need flow forth from Him.

So often our lives seem to be like the shifting sands. Circumstances around us change continually. We are dealing with our jobs, our crowded schedules and maintaining our homes. We are trying to take care of our families and to foster our relationships with our friends and church families. And we are also trying to grow in God, to have a vibrant prayer life, to grow in the Word, to minister to others as the Lord leads. Life can get to be overwhelming at times. But when it does, we have a place to turn:

> *From the end of the earth will I cry unto thee,*
> *when my heart is overwhelmed: lead me to the*
> *rock that is higher than I.*   Psalm 61:2

Like the coney, we can flee to the Rock for safety and shelter. The Rock is stable. It is solid, firm, strong, and secure. The rocks the coney dwells in are permanent, not easily moved or carried away.

I need a hiding place that is permanent too. I need a refuge that is sure, one that I don't have to chase after, running to find it. I need a dwelling that is secure, that will be ready for me in my time of need.

And I have one. I find my refuge in the Rock. The presence of the Lord my God is my place of escape and healing. And He is yours as well.

Ours is a troublesome world. It is chaotic, full of pain. But we have a means of escape when we run to the presence of the Lord:

> *Thou wilt show me the path of life: in thy presence is fulness of joy; at thy right hand there are pleasures for evermore.* Psalm 16:11

Jesus is the Rock of all ages. He is steadfast. He cannot be moved. He was *"tempted in all points, yet without sin."* The grave could not hold Him down, and the cross could not finish Him. He was raised from the dead and is alive forevermore. Truly we can place our trust in Him, for He is our Fortress and our Deliverer:

> *The eternal God is thy refuge, and underneath are the everlasting arms: and he shall thrust out the enemy from before thee; and shall say, Destroy them.* Deuteronomy 33:27

The eternal God, the everlasting God, is our Protector. Yes, we are weak, but we are supported by His *"everlasting arms."* The prophet Isaiah confirms this:

Taking Refuge in the Rock

Fear thou not; for I am with thee: be not dismayed;
for I am thy God: I will strengthen thee; yea, I
will help thee; yea, I will uphold thee with the right
hand of my righteousness. Isaiah 41:10

If you are facing a crisis, be glad. If God is bringing you face to face with your weakness, rejoice. This is God's opportunity to reveal His power in you and through you. It is in the midst of obscurity that the glory of God can shine forth in all its brightness:

For in the time of trouble he shall hide me in his
pavilion: in the secret of his tabernacle shall he
hide me; he shall set me up upon a rock.
Psalm 27:5

The Pavilion was part of the Temple, and the glory of God's anointed presence dwelt there. It is so good to know that in our time of trouble, God will hide us in His Pavilion — in His glory, in His anointing, in His presence, in His grace, in His power!

We serve a great God, and when trouble comes, the anointing of His presence will be my hiding place. He is ready to show Himself strong on behalf of His people, whom He has called to Himself. And we are blessed to be a part of that company of people who can be hidden in Him.

God is never too late. He is never in a hurry. He is always on time. In our times of trouble, He is there.

In our times of danger, He is there. In our times of need, He is there.

David declared:

> *God is our refuge and strength, a very present help in trouble. Therefore will not we fear, though the earth be removed, and though the mountains be carried into the midst of the sea; though the waters thereof roar and be troubled, though the mountains shake with the swelling thereof. Selah.*
>
> Psalm 46:1-3

He is *"very present"* to help us. It doesn't matter what the experts say — the economists, the politicians, the news media. Whatever the crisis, God will hide us. And in the presence of the Lord there is no need or lack. Find your refuge and shelter in God. Find yourself in the arms of the Lord.

The Bible tells us that Jesus wept over Jerusalem, crying out:

> *O Jerusalem, Jerusalem, which killest the prophets, and stonest them that are sent unto thee; how often would I have gathered thy children together, as a hen doth gather her brood under her wings, and ye would not!*
>
> Luke 13:34

What a tragedy for the people of that time! *"How often would I have gathered you ... and ye would not!"*

Let us not make this same mistake. Allow yourself to be gathered in. Come under the wings of God's presence, the anointing of His power, the gifts of His grace. Be covered by the blood and life of the Lord Jesus. Only He can be a true refuge. All others will fail. There is nothing else in which we can place our trust. No one is infallible. God alone is able to keep His promise of safety and peace. He alone is our Rock.

God has promised that whenever we are in trouble and we look to Him, He will send His angels to save and deliver us. We can know security, peace and contentment in God, just as a child knows these things when he is held in his parents' arms:

But as many as received him, to them gave he power to become the sons of God, even to them that believe on his name: which were born, not of blood, nor of the will of the flesh, nor of the will of man, but of God. John 1:12-13

But when the fulness of the time was come, God sent forth his Son, made of a woman, made under the law, to redeem them that were under the law, that we might receive the adoption of sons. And because ye are sons, God hath sent forth the Spirit of his Son into your hearts, crying, Abba, Father. Galatians 4:4-6

When we are born again, we are birthed into the family of God. Just as a small child will willingly go wherever his father leads him as long as that father is holding his hand, so should be with us. As a child seeks refuge and healing in his mother's arms when he has fallen and scraped his knee, so are we to seek the refuge of our Parent when we have been hurt. As a parent does, God will hold us closely while He works to clean and dress our wounds. He will whisper His words of love in our ears as He comforts us. His love and care for us is that of a parent for a child, and, like children, we can trust Him implicitly.

What does Jesus say to us?

> *Come unto me, all ye that labour and are heavy laden, and I will give you rest. Take my yoke upon you, and learn of me; for I am meek and lowly in heart: and ye shall find rest unto your souls. For my yoke is easy, and my burden is light.*
>
> Matthew 11:28-30

You are in the arms of the One who has loved you *"with an everlasting love."* You are being embraced by the One who has called you forth to be His son, His daughter. Remember that your Father is a Giver. He gives good gifts to His children, and He is not stingy or selfish. His nature is to give more than to receive, to minister more than to be ministered to.

Whatever you are going through, know that your

Father in Heaven is your Hiding Place. In Him you will find safety, tranquility and sweet rest. Whatever the difficulty, run swiftly, like the coney, to *"the Rock that is higher than [you]."* His love for you endures. It is always fresh and new.

God doesn't forget about us, He doesn't neglect us, and His Word promises that He will always receive us into His arms:

For he hath said, I will never leave thee, nor forsake thee.   Hebrews 13:5

Teaching them to observe all things whatsoever I have commanded you: and, lo, I am with you alway, even unto the end of the world. Amen.
                                                           Matthew 28:20

Our Lord is with us always, to protect us in our weakness because of His great love for us. Don't be guilty of running from the Lord. Run to Him. Run from your weakness to His strength. Run from your sickness to His health. Run from your problems to His solutions.

Run to the Lord; cling to Him; and find yourself protected and preserved by His love.

In the eyes of your enemy you are insignificant and helpless, and he will try to intimidate you by making you compare yourself to him. But stop comparing yourself to anyone or anything else and start looking to the Rock. Find you significance in Him.

Without the Rock you are nothing, but in Him you can do all things. With His protection you cannot fail.

Learn the wisdom of the coney. He is feeble, and he is limited, but he knows where to hide. Look to your Refuge. Know that the Rock is your Strength. And run swiftly to Him.

PART FOUR:

THE LOCUST

7

DISCOVERING THE
POWER OF UNITY

The locusts have no king, yet go they forth all of them by bands.　　　　　　　Proverbs 30:27

How this insignificant creature could put the Church to shame! *"The locusts have no king."* They have no leader. They have no captain. They have no pastor. They have no elders, no deacons, no overseers. They have no Sunday school teachers or greeters or ushers. But they do have one thing that seems to be sorely lacking in the Church, something for which Christ prayed at the end of His earthly ministry — unity for all believers.

There is no one to tell the locusts what to do. There is none to give them direction. Still, they work and travel together. Not one is left out: *"They go forth all of them by bands."* Locusts are a model of a group that is united in purpose and vision and that knows how to work together.

Locusts move as one. I have never seen a group of locusts holding a discussion to determine the future direction of the group. I have never seen them holding an election. They are a model of teamwork. And if these creatures can function successfully that way, then we humans should be able to do even better.

Although the locusts have no king, they go forward in unity. They work together in harmony. We desperately need those qualities in the Body of Christ. We have our pastors, elders, committees, boards, presbyteries and department heads. We have so many people whose job it is to ensure that there is a common vision and purpose, but still we cannot get along together. Still the Body of Christ is divided.

Locusts don't have these problems. They don't divide themselves over their beliefs, their doctrines, their personality differences. In fact, it is difficult to find a locust by himself. They seem to understand a truth the Church has yet to grasp: alone they can do very little. Alone, a locust has very little impact, very little power to change anything; but when locusts

;ravel with other locusts, there is a great change in this situation. They arrive in a large battalion and eat everything in sight. In a large group, they can effect major changes. Their impact will be seen, and feared, by all.

Alone, the locust is nothing, but with a group he becomes somebody. In unity there is strength, power and ability to carry out the vision. When we are united, no one is overworked, because everyone is helping to carry out the responsibility in maintaining orderliness, peace and unity within the family.

Church, it is time to rise up and to be united, joined with one another. As this happens, your strength becomes my strength, and my strength becomes your strength. No one is weak, because we each supply what is lacking in the other members. We need to live our lives as a community and as a family.

Look into your life. Are there barriers that keep you from deeper fellowship with other believers? What is it that is holding you back? Often it is some sin from the past, some skeleton in the closet. We are afraid that others might see what we are "really" like. But if you have given that thing over to the Lord Jesus, allowing Him to cleanse you in His blood, then that skeleton is no longer there. It has been done away with in God. We have nothing to fear, and nothing to hide.

I can open the door of my life and let you come

in, because all you will see is Jesus. Yes, I have weaknesses, limitations, inabilities; but if you come into my life, you will discover that in the absence of the things that I may need, there is the sufficiency of God's grace working in me. You will marvel that despite my weaknesses, God has become my sufficiency. He is working in my life for His glory and honor. Despite the shortcomings, we can see the grace of God moving in the lives of each believer.

Don't be a faultfinder. Instead, help people to overcome their faults. Don't criticize, but help others to overcome their weaknesses. Don't be the one pulling your brothers and sisters down, but the one pulling them up. We are one Body and one family.

Too often everyone is *"doing what is right in his own eyes,"* everyone going in his own direction. There is a spirit of independence which encourages this type of relating — or nonrelating. There is an attitude afoot in the Church that says, "If you don't mind me, I don't mind you. If you will leave me alone, I'll leave you alone." But that mind-set is from the devil. So is this classic question: "Why don't you mind your own business?"

Well, I have news for you: If you are a member of the Body of Christ, you *are* my business, and I am your business. You had better see to it that I'm taken care of, and I had better see to it that you're taken care of.

If we are part of the Body of Christ, then we are

connected. Paul explained this in a letter to the church at Corinth:

> *For as the body is one, and hath many members, and all the members of that one body, being many, are one body: so also is Christ. For by one Spirit are we all baptized into one body, whether we be Jews or Gentiles, whether we be bond or free; and have been all made to drink into one Spirit. For the body is not one member, but many. ... Now ye are the body of Christ, and members in particular.*
>
> 1 Corinthians 12:12-14 and 27

As believers, we are all part of the same Body, with Christ as our Head. Because of this, there is to be caring for one another, an empathy that ties us together. Paul wrote of this also in describing how the Body is to function:

> *And whether one member suffer, all the members suffer with it; or one member be honoured, all the members rejoice with it.*   1 Corinthians 12:26

Too often there is a lack of this type of caring one for another within the Body of Christ. When we do not care for one another, support one another and encourage one another, then we are not truly walking in love with one another. When we are not walking in love, there is bound to be discord. And where there is discord, the Body of our Lord is divided.

This is not pleasing to God! We are not to divide the Body, the Church. We are to walk in love with one another, understanding that we are mutually connected, that we have been supernaturally joined together by our Lord. We are to be as one, functioning in unity, caring for one another, counting others as more important than ourselves:

> *Let nothing be done through strife or vainglory; but in lowliness of mind let each esteem other better than themselves.* Philippians 2:3

We are to see others as more important, or "*better*," than ourselves. Why would that be? Is it to make us feel inferior? No. It is so that we gain a proper measure of ourselves. It is so that we don't raise ourselves up as being more than we are.

One problem many local churches have in this regard is that small groups form within the churches, but not for the purpose of edification. These are groups of people with something in common, who band together in keeping others out of their little group. Another word for such a group is a *clique*.

Cliques are divisions within the church. They are small groups that attempt to dictate who may relate to whom. People in cliques do not reach out to others in the church. And Heaven help the visitor or new member who wants to fellowship with these people! It cannot be done. The members of these groups have built walls against others who might want to come into their group. Often there is a spirit of self-righteousness among the members of these groups, who may share pet doctrines or teachings. Spoken or not, the feeling that the clique is more spiritual, more intellectual or otherwise better than others is often present.

Brothers and sisters, this should not be! We are to look to others as "*better*" than ourselves, not raise ourselves up as patterns and standards to be followed. There should be no barriers among the people of God, for we are one family. Within the Church, there are no rich and no poor, no educated and uneducated. We are one in the Lord. Let us not try to divide the Church of our God. Rather, let us work to unite the Body:

> *Till we all come in the unity of the faith, and of the knowledge of the Son of God, unto a perfect man, unto the measure of the stature of the fulness of Christ.* Ephesians 4:13

We are all to be united. Therefore, let us encourage one another; let us treat one another with kindness and courtesy and compassion; let us love one another as Christ has commanded us to do.

Although we are all part of the same Body, we

are not all alike. Nor should we try to be. There should be unity, but this is to be the true unity of the Spirit of God, not a false unity based on conformity. As members of the Body, we have a variety of giftings, functions and responsibilities.

> *But now hath God set the members every one of them in the body, as it hath pleased him. And if they were all one member, where were the body? But now are they many members, yet but one body. And the eye cannot say unto the hand, I have no need of thee: nor again the head to the feet, I have no need of you.*
>
> 1 Corinthians 12:18-21

There are no insignificant members in the Body. Although we are all different, each has a specific function and each must recognize his or her significance in order for the entire Body to function properly.

Although we function differently, we are each important in God's program, and we each know that God has a plan for our lives. He has a destiny and a will for every one of us.

Part of that will includes caring for our brothers and sisters in the Lord. It was the guilty murderer Cain who cried out, "Am I my brother's keeper?" And it is the Spirit of the Lord who answers a resounding, "Yes! I have placed you together with others within My Church, that you may care for one another, growing in love. I have given you each one the other as a gift, that you may begin to learn what it means to live in My Kingdom, walking in unity and love — even when you disagree."

We are responsible for one another. The Word of God tells us how we are to relate to others in the family of believers:

And let us consider one another to provoke unto love and to good works. Hebrews 10:24

Be kindly affectioned one to another with brotherly love; in honour preferring one another.
Romans 12:10

For, brethren, ye have been called unto liberty; only use not liberty for an occasion to the flesh, but by love serve one another. Galatians 5:13

And be ye kind one to another, tenderhearted, forgiving one another, even as God for Christ's sake hath forgiven you. Ephesians 4:32

Wherefore comfort yourselves together, and edify one another, even as also ye do.
1 Thessalonians 5:11

Not forsaking the assembling of ourselves together, as the manner of some is; but exhorting one an-

> *other: and so much the more, as ye see the day*
> *approaching.* Hebrews 10:25

> *This is My commandment, That ye love one an-*
> *other, as I have loved you.* John 15:12

The Bible contains many of these "*one another*" verses. Interestingly, quite a few exhort believers to "*love one another.*" It seems that if we obey this commandment, our obedience to all the others will flow from that first obedience.

The underlying teaching of these verses is that we must be able to get along with one another, to work together in the Kingdom of God to accomplish His purposes — without personalities and quarrels intruding in the process.

How are we to accomplish this? How are we to truly "*be at peace with all men*"? It isn't easy. It requires sacrifice. It is called "*dying to self.*"

The death of our flesh is not something we like to contemplate. Repentance and the dying to self are not generally the most popular of topics for sermons, but they are important. Unless we are dying to self and to sin, unless we are preferring others above ourselves, unless we are repenting and making things right with our brothers and sisters, we will not be able to know and experience all that God has for us in this move of the Holy Spirit. We cannot walk in unity with others if we are not walking in unity with God.

Discovering the Power of Unity

It was Paul who wrote of the death to self:

I am crucified with Christ: nevertheless I live; yet not I, but Christ liveth in me: and the life which I now live in the flesh I live by the faith of the Son of God, who loved me, and gave himself for me.

Galatians 2:20

This crucified life is not simply a onetime experience. It is a continual walking out of death to the flesh, or self, that longs to do as it pleases. Paul also wrote:

I die daily.   1 Corinthians 15:31

This is the key to success in the Christian life. It is the only means by which we can walk in unity with others for longer than it takes to have the first disagreement.

Locusts don't have the Holy Spirit. They don't have the Word of God to guide them. They don't have a place of worship. They have no pastors to oversee them, yet they have a spirit of unity and harmony. Locusts work together as a team.

We seem to have a lot to learn about teamwork. Working together as a team means laying aside our personal goals and agendas to seek the best for the group. There is a certain death to self that is involved if the team is to succeed. But the sacrifice of my own goals and ambitions is worth it. Why? Because if the team wins, I win too, since I am part of the team. It costs me little, therefore, to lay aside my personal concerns for the sake of the whole team. Individuality no longer carries the same importance. It's the team that counts.

We need individual players on the team, but we are no longer individuals, with individual goals and tastes. We are a team, working together, our eyes fixed on a common goal, and that is to win. Winning is the team's obsession.

What position you play doesn't matter. What is important is that you work together with those with whom God has placed you as a team. Don't get discouraged when you are out of play for a while. Pursue the Lord's work in your life at those times, knowing that He is training and perfecting you, readying you for His use. Be ready to minister at a moment's notice. We are all working together for the expansion of the Kingdom of God.

We see these principles at work frequently in many sports, where teamwork is necessary. We see them at work in many places of business, as a teamwork mentality is fostered among workers that is to benefit the entire company. We need to see it much more in the Church.

Too often we see a grasping after position and authority within local churches. People are so busy looking out for themselves and for their own interests that those who need to be cared for are left behind. There is also a spirit of competition. One ministry is exalted above another, when only One is to be exalted by the Church — the One who died for us, who earnestly prayed that all believers might be one with Him and with one another.

When locusts move, none is ahead and none is behind. They all move together. No one is pushing and shoving. No one is grabbing. Each instinctively understands the other's position. There is no argument about it either. Without any leader to whip them into shape, locusts show discipline and form themselves into orderly ranks. They don't need lengthy instruction. They are guided by common, unseen forces.

Locusts are not haughty, looking down on some of their members while lifting up others. This needs to be reality in the life of the Church as well. Every local church is full of seemingly insignificant, unimportant and unnoticed people. They are not in the spotlight. They hold no visible position within the church structure. But they are not insignificant — either to God or to the life of the church itself. These people are doing great things for God, even though they are not recognized by men.

When we seek to advance within the church and to be recognized, that's carnality. When we begin to promote ourselves so that we can be placed into a certain position, that's worldliness. But godliness is entirely different. Godliness seeks to obey the voice of the Lord. Godliness is willing to serve, to quietly encourage, to minister out of sight of the people. And people with this godly heart will do great and lasting things in the Kingdom of God.

Generally speaking, most of those who are living godly lives are not holding offices or recognized positions of authority in the church. What is important is that they are living lives of faith. These are people of integrity and honesty, sometimes more so than those set into places of leadership.

But even though they are qualified, these godly people are not seeking any position, recognition or applause. Their hearts are to serve the Lord. I believe that if we had more people like those in our churches today, we would see more unity. We would know more harmony. We would experience revival, and our churches would be packed with people.

Can we have such wisdom? Can we lay hold of godliness? Can we cease from our fruitless arguing and grasping after position to move as one with those whom Christ has given us to walk with and work with?

After Christ's ascension, the disciples returned to Jerusalem, as He had bid them. And then they waited ten days. Have you ever wondered why the disciples had to wait ten days in the Upper Room before the Spirit of God descended upon them? That's a long time to wait in the same place, if you think about it. I believe that for the first few days they were together "*in one place,*" but it was only after some days of waiting and praying they were also "*in one accord.*" It was then that the Spirit descended upon them. Personally, I believe that if they had never gotten into unity of spirit, God's power would not have been manifested.

There is strength in agreement. The Word of God says:

> *Again I say unto you, That if two of you shall agree on earth as touching any thing that they shall ask, it shall be done for them of my Father which is in heaven.* Matthew 18:19

There is power in unity. When your heart is united with your brother, God honors that. Godly unity brings an anointing from the Lord.

> *Behold, how good and how pleasant it is for brethren to dwell together in unity! It is like the precious ointment upon the head, that ran down upon the beard, even Aaron's beard: that went down to the skirts of his garments.* Psalm 133:1-2

Just like the locusts, God has designed us, His "new creation," to "*dwell together in unity.*" We don't always realize it and act that way, but He has given us His life, His Spirit, His Word, His guidance, everything we need to be able to live in this way.

Independent people have a lot to learn. They may accomplish something alone, but if they joined their forces with others, they could do much more.

We are to care for one another in the Body, meeting each other's needs as we work together in the plan and purpose of God. Rather than criticizing and finding fault with one another, we need to pray for our brothers and sisters:

> *Blessed is the man that walketh not in the counsel of the ungodly, nor standeth in the way of sinners, nor sitteth in the seat of the scornful.*
>
> Psalm 1:1

We are "*blessed*" if we do not "*sit in the seat of the scornful*," looking down on others, criticizing our brothers and sisters. Yet we hear such things all the time. "Did you hear that last sermon? I never can follow what he's trying to say. I wonder if he'll ever learn to teach." "I wish they hadn't given her that solo. I could do it much better." Or the ever-popular, "Could you pray with me about this situation? Don't let it get out, but ..."

Brothers and sisters, such things should not be found among us. Our words can tear apart the Body of our Lord!

When you say or do something against a member of the Body, you are doing it against yourself. There is no way you can separate yourself from the whole and prosper. The responsibility of the strong is to strengthen the weak, not to push them down further.

Stop looking for recognition, for position. That is where these kinds of problems come from. We want others to notice us, to approve of us, to look up to us. This may be natural, but it's not godly.

When I think about who I am in God, I really don't care whether anyone recognizes me or not. Who I am in Him is enough to make me rejoice. When I look back and see where God found me, when I look at where He has brought me from and where He is taking me, it is enough. How exciting!

I don't need the adulation of men to tell me I'm important. I know my significance in God. I'm not hungry for recognition because I know that God recognizes me. I'm not hungry for position because I know that God will put me in the best possible position. I am *"seated in heavenly places with Christ Jesus"* (see Ephesians 2:6). There is no better position than that!

As we walk in unity, harmony and agreement, with everyone working in one accord, we will enter into a new realm of possibility of what we can do in God. Are you ready to enter into that realm? Are you ready to die to yourself and to your own desires, ambitions and goals? Are you ready to be wise like the locust?

8

Having One Purpose

With all lowliness and meekness, with longsuffer-
ing, forbearing one another in love; endeavouring
to keep the unity of the Spirit in the bond of peace.
There is one body, and one Spirit, even as ye are
called in one hope of your calling; one Lord, one
faith, one baptism, one God and Father of all, who
is above all, and through all, and in you all.

Ephesians 4:2-6

It is good to be walking in unity, caring for one another, fellowshiping with one another, preferring others above oneself, but there is another aspect of unity that the locust can show us: unity of purpose. The prophet Amos asked:

Can two walk together, except they be agreed?
                                        Amos 3:3

It does us no good to be relating well and loving one another if we are not going anywhere. Some groups seem to specialize in this type of relationship.

Once relationships are in place, all the ministries are functioning and everyone's needs are being met, they heave a sigh of relief. Then they enter maintenance mode. Nothing new happens. No one reaches out to the lost. No one seeks new direction from the Lord for the church. They simply strive to maintain what they have built. Such a church may look good, but it is going nowhere.

We need to be people of vision, people of purpose. We need to be those who set our eyes on accomplishing what God has for us to do. If you have no vision, no definite point of destination, you may be just stumbling around in the dark. You are like a boat without a sail, drifting on life's seas. That is very dangerous.

The locusts have a sense of purpose. They know their destination, even though they have no designated leader among them. They are concentrated on their purpose: finding something substantial to eat. The whole group travels together pursuing that common purpose.

Although no one tells them what to do, the locusts are in agreement. They rely on their instincts, in a sense, to tell them what they are to be doing. They rely on an inner "knowing," an inner "voice," if you will. They listen to the sounds borne on the wind, they feel the direction of the breeze as it passes by them, and they look for an abundance of food — enough to feed them all.

As believers, we can learn from the example of the locust. Although we have no earthly king, we can go forth by bands as we listen to the voice of the Holy Spirit. As we are alert to what is going on in the world around us, as we look to the Lord, we can go forward as one.

We each have an individual purpose. There are individual plans and goals, specific destinies set into our lives and hearts by God. But there are also some things we all have in common.

For instance, I know that God's will for your life and for mine is that we be transformed "*into the image and likeness of His Son,*" Jesus Christ. Our glorious destiny is to shine forth the beauty of Jesus Christ and to become "*the light of the world.*" We are to maintain the flavor of the life of Christ in us so that we become "*the salt of the earth.*" Our destiny is that we should be the epistles of God, that the world would see Jesus in us. It's not how we speak that matters; it's how we live out the Word of God. It's not how loud we shout that's important; it's with what purity we live our lives.

The Lord will accomplish these things in different ways in our lives, and He will use us in different areas of ministry; but the basic purpose and goal is still the same. We are to be changed into His likeness. Let us pursue that goal:

> *I press toward the mark for the prize of the high calling of God in Christ Jesus.* Philippians 3:14

Just as there is an individual purpose for our lives, there is also a corporate purpose for the life of the local church. Every church should have a vision, a purpose for existing, a destination to which we can chart our course. And just as there are common goals for each of us, so there are visions which should be shared by all the churches.

Every church should have the goal of being a place where its people can learn to commune with God through prayer and through worship. Each local body should be a soul-winning church, a church that will raise up men and women to go out into the towns and cities, across the nation and around the world, to win the lost. And each church should be making disciples of the new believers and training its people to be disciplers as well. Each church will then lift up the name of Jesus and show the world that He truly is Lord.

These are wonderful goals, God-glorifying goals, but we cannot accomplish any of them unless each of us catches the same vision and is willing to move forward with it.

Having One Purpose

God has formed each local church for a purpose. Let us not allow the devil to hinder us in accomplishing that purpose. Let us allow no personal ambition to stand in the way of our marching forward, united, to the goal.

How will we best accomplish the task that God has set before us? It can only be accomplished as we move together in unity. A lone insect makes a quiet sound as it flies, but when a cloud of locusts approaches, they make such a loud noise that everyone hears them coming from a long way off. We might even think the sound was from an approaching airplane. That's the type of impact God's people can have when they are united in purpose and spirit:

For the kingdom of God is not in word, but in power.   1 Corinthians 4:20

Our sound is to be like that of a mighty army marching to war.

After a swarm of locusts has been in a place and has gone on, you will notice the impact. Any vegetation that had been there is gone. You will see by the evidence left behind that the locusts are powerful creatures, and the source of their strength and power is found in their unity.

This is how the Church is to be. Our strength lies in our being *"in one accord."* Our power lies in our being of *"one mind"* and *"heart,"* our respecting one another, our recognizing the gifts of others. We are to be united in purpose, having clarity of vision and going forth in the name of the Lord to bring forth His Kingdom.

Vision is powerful:

> *Where there is no vision, the people perish: but he that keepeth the law, happy is he.*
>
> Proverbs 29:18

Vision is just as important to the individual as it is to the Church. Without vision we will die – as a church or as an individual. Why? Because without a clear vision for what the local church is to be doing or for why it began in the first place, each member will be going in a different direction, trying to do whatever he thinks should be done. And though the goals of each member may be worthy, if each person is pulling in a different direction, the Body will eventually be pulled apart. A corporate vision allows believers to know where they are going. It helps visitors to see whether a particular local church is where the Lord desires them to be. Can their giftings and abilities be used of the Lord in this particular local church? Can the call of God on their lives be integrated with the ministry and outreach style of this body of believers?

We need to pray, "God, bring us into a place where we can say we're all one, one voice, one body." There may be many members, and there may be many differences among those members, but we are still one Body. As we recognize that we are one, we are able to accomplish that which God has called us to do:

Finally, be ye all of one mind, having compassion one of another, love as brethren, be pitiful, be courteous.   1 Peter 3:8

"*Love one another as brothers.*" We disagree at times, but our love for one another overcomes the anger, preventing bitterness from laying hold and taking root in the heart.

We are to care for one another, carrying the burdens of others:

Bear ye one another's burdens, and so fulfil the law of Christ.   Galatians 6:2

And as we bear those burdens, caring for one another, the Lord is building us together into a Temple for His dwelling:

Now therefore ye are no more strangers and foreigners, but fellowcitizens with the saints, and of the household of God; and are built upon the foundation of the apostles and prophets, Jesus Christ Himself being the chief corner stone; in whom all the building fitly framed together groweth unto

an holy temple in the Lord: in whom ye also are
builded together for an habitation of God through
the Spirit.   Ephesians 2:19-22

We are "*fitly framed together,*" no longer "*strangers*" to one another. We have unity of purpose, going forth together to accomplish the will of the Lord, having laid hold of the vision of the Lord for our local churches.

Let us seek the Lord to see what He wants to accomplish in each locality, what direction the ministry should take. And then let us walk forward into that vision as He directs.

Often, even if there is a general plan for a church, there isn't a consensus on how to actually walk out that vision. There may be a goal, but no one has laid out a clear path for getting to the goal. Again we can learn from the locust.

You never see locusts arguing about which way they should go. They don't leave one place for another unless everyone is ready to leave. There are no stragglers left behind.

There is an emphasis throughout the Bible, and especially in the New Testament, on our being one. We are one Body, so we are to move as one. In the natural, if you see someone whose body is not functioning properly — perhaps the legs will not move together to enable him to walk, or the neck muscles will not properly support the head — then you know that something is not right. Perhaps there has been an accident, or a disease has harmed the person's body.

In the spirit, it is the same. If the ministries do not function together properly, or if the church is not moving forward, or the members are not supporting one another; if you see that the body is not functioning properly, then you know that something is not right.

Let us not just be of "*one Body,*" but let us also be "*of one mind,*" "*one heart*" and one purpose. Let "*the mind of Christ*" be in each of us:

> *And be not conformed to this world: but be ye transformed by the renewing of your mind, that ye may prove what is that good, and acceptable, and perfect, will of God.* Romans 12:2

We are all "*members one of another*":

> *We, being many, are one body in Christ, and every one members one of another.* Romans 12:5

Each believer is a part of the other believers. So we need one another. We cannot live alone. We cannot mature in God as hermits. We need the other members of the Body of Christ.

Would you intentionally cut off your own hand, or a foot? Do you think you could easily do without your mouth, or your lungs or your heart? In the natural, we need all the members of our bodies — no matter how insignificant each may seem. In fact, the Scriptures declare:

> *And those members of the body, which we think to be less honourable, upon these we bestow more abundant honour; and our uncomely parts have more abundant comeliness. For our comely parts have no need: but God hath tempered the body together, having given more abundant honour to that part which lacked: that there should be no schism in the body; but that the members should have the same care one for another. And whether one member suffer, all the members suffer with it; or one member be honoured, all the members re-joice with it.*   1 Corinthians 12:23-26

Some members seem great and others small, but they all are important to God.

Just as the physical body needs all of its various parts, so it is in the spiritual as well. We need one another. Each has a designated role, and each is important to the other.

What happens when you try to hammer a nail into a piece of wood and miss? There is immediate pain! And what does your body do? Does it hold a committee meeting to determine whether to do anything for your throbbing thumb? No! Immediately your other hand drops the hammer to hold and soothe the hurt thumb. In the same way, we are to care for others, for they are part of the Body of which we are members.

Finally, let us esteem one another as *"fellow heirs"* with Christ. There is only one means of salvation, through our Lord Jesus Christ and by His shed blood.

> *For we being many are one bread, and one body:*
> *for we are all partakers of that one bread.*
>   1 Corinthians 10:17

There is only one Savior. There is only one truth. There is only one cross. There is only one door and one life. We came into the Kingdom of God by grace, and neither you nor I have anything of which to boast. We must lay aside our pride and our boasting to come together in the purposes of God.

How do we achieve this coming together in God? First, we must respect one another, and we must see each person as a unique creation of God. Is there a person in your life with whom it is difficult for you to get along? Does someone seem to know just the wrong time to show up, the wrong thing to say? You probably have someone like this in your life. We all do at times, for the Lord uses these kinds of relationships to help us to grow and mature. We are living stones, and sometimes it takes the rubbing of stone against stone to knock off the rough edges.

Know that these "difficult" people are placed by God into your life. And just as you are important to God, the result of the Divine imagination, so is that other person with whom you have no patience, toward whom you have so little respect. We must not look at people's past mistakes, binding them to those sins or errors: "How can we trust him?" some ask. "We know how he always did." We must walk in forgiveness, and respect one another as forgiven creatures of God.

Sometimes we respect people because of the things they put on their bodies — the clothes, the jewelry, the accessories. Sometimes we look at people's occupations. Does it really matter if a person is a doctor or a lawyer or a janitor? We're all children of God. Believers are all one in the Lord. We need to respect everyone. We are to love everybody, receiving and accepting them in the name of the Lord.

Respect is important in all of our relationships with others. We can see it in marriages. When the husband respects the wife and the wife respects the husband, there will be unity, harmony, love and fellowship. In homes where this respect exists, you won't see plates flying through the air like Frisbees!

There should be respect between parents and children, not just from children to parents, but also from the parents to the children. Don't take the attitude that children have no right to voice an opinion. The parents have the authority, yes, but that authority is to be exercised in an atmosphere of love and caring.

Our children are the creation of God, and He has a destiny for them. We can either support it and help them to fulfill it, or we can tear it down and help to destroy their lives. Love your children the way you ought to love them. Respect them the way you ought to respect them. Build them up instead of tearing them down. Motivate them; encourage them. Stir them to excel in the Lord in everything they do. Children are gifts, blessings from God.

Each of us wants to be respected. Respect gives us a sense of worth and value. But respect is something we have to earn. It is not freely given. If you prove yourself worthy of respect, everyone will respect you. If you want to be respected, be respectable. Show forth integrity of character, walk out what you say you believe, and have a spirit of humility rather than boasting — if you want to be respected.

May the Spirit of God bind His people together, as families and as congregations, for the glory of the Lord. May we go forward as one — one in vision, one in unity and one in purpose. May we have respect for one another, realizing that each member of the Body of Christ is important, created by God. And may we walk in love in such a way as to bring glory and honor to our Lord.

Jesus said:

By this shall all men know that ye are my disciples, if ye have love one to another. John 13:35

In the spirit of unity of purpose and of vision, we can find our significance, both as individuals and as congregations. In following the same spirit of unity witnessed among the locusts, we can go forth to build up God's Kingdom in love. I say to young and old alike, you can have a significant impact on your world as you discover your true significance in God.

PART FIVE:

THE SPIDER

9

CLEAVING TO YOUR GOAL

The spider taketh hold with her hands, and is in kings' palaces.   Proverbs 30:28

The Lord must really enjoy spiders — after all, He created some six hundred different species of them. Scientists have even determined that we are rarely more than three feet away from a spider. Now, that's a plentiful creature! And we know that God made them all for a purpose. They are not here only to eat harmful insects, but to give us a wonderful lesson.

Most people consider spiders to be ugly, even frightening. They find very little of beauty in spiders. These creatures are rarely kept as pets. Few people like the idea of having a spider in bed with them. In fact, many people scream when they see a spider, or they run in the other direction. Spiders simply are not well liked by most people.

We see this dislike in our culture. For instance, if you read in a book that someone is "spider-like" in his manner, or if his shadow on the wall looks like a spider, you know right away that he is not to be trusted. He is the bad guy, who will try to lure the innocent victim into his clutches.

Some of this distrust may be due to the odd appearance of spiders. Unlike insects, who have three body sections, spiders have only two — head and abdomen. Rather than having six legs like insects, spiders have eight legs.

Spiders are very frail. Their legs look too thin for their bodies. They wiggle. They wobble. They have little strength. A spider cannot even walk unless it pumps blood into its legs to straighten them. When the blood circulates back out, the legs bend again. There is very little substance to them.

Spiders remind me of malnourished children. They have big stomachs, but all the other parts of their bodies are small, and out of proportion. I wonder sometimes how spiders can be so thin and yet still survive.

Yet despite their poor reputation and their appearance, most spiders are small and fairly easy to catch. If their webs are struck violently, spiders usually don't have the strength to stay on them.

But spiders have an amazing defense. If they are confronted or their space is defiled, they don't give up. They don't just crawl away in disgust and say, "Well, so much for that." After a few disturbances in one spot, they don't even rebuild their webs in the place where they were disturbed. So, what do they do? They simply climb up higher and make a new web in a safer place.

Our scripture tells us that the spider "*taketh hold with her hands.*" She holds on tightly, not letting go.

There are very few places to which a spider cannot go. Anchoring herself, she can use her web-making skill to get her from place to place. She is a good climber and jumper as well. Her web serves as a safety net for her, enabling her to crawl without fear. If she falls, she can climb back up on her web.

The spider has a vision, a goal. I noticed this when I was growing up. Sometimes spiders made webs in places that were not convenient for us, so we would remove the web in the morning. But by the following day, there would be another web. Again we would remove it, and again it would appear the next morning. If we knocked it down several times, the spider would move to another corner and begin to make another web — where no one could find it or bother it.

The spider doesn't stop spinning her webs even if there are obstacles, opposition or enemies that come against her. Why not? Because she has a goal.

Her vision is to climb to the highest possible altitude — where insects fly freely.

The Word of God says that the spider can even be found "*in kings' palaces.*" Spiders can aspire to live in the dwellings of kings. They can witness all the pomp and glory that accompanies royalty. And they can live in the midst of it.

We also have a call to a higher life. We don't have to be satisfied with our present level of achievement. We can aspire to greater things. Don't be content to live in low places. We are called to come up to the dwelling of the King. Why be content to survive in a hut when there is a palace waiting for you?

The palace in which the spider lives is one that will eventually be destroyed, but the Bible tells us of a "*mansion*" that God is building in the city where there will be no night, no darkness, and where the light will be "*the Lamb*" of God:

> *And I saw no temple therein: for the Lord God Almighty and the Lamb are the temple of it. And the city had no need of the sun, neither of the moon, to shine in it: for the glory of God did lighten it, and the Lamb is the light thereof.*
>
> Revelation 21:22-23

The gates of that city will be made of pearl, and the streets of pure gold. It will be worth withstanding the opposition. It will be worth the sacrifice, the battle, the suffering. Most important of all, we will see Him! So let us fix our minds and hearts on our goal. And let us remember the spider. Because of her dream, her vision, her goal, she is able to live in kings' palaces.

Because of their vision and goals, spiders have an attitude of persistence. They don't sit down in a corner feeling sorry for themselves because their web was destroyed. They set themselves to begin a new web. They are persistent in all their endeavors.

Have you gone through some difficult times in your spiritual life? Too many are willing to say, "I'm sorry, Lord, but it's just too hard. Good-bye." But your life will be even more difficult if you turn it over to the devil. Backsliding is not something you want to consider. Instead, turn and embrace your Lord. See His face, and seek His grace.

Even if you suffer and go through difficulties, the Lord is there. His *"grace is sufficient"* for you, and His *"mercies endure forever."* He *"will never leave you nor forsake you,"* but He will be with you *"even to the end of the age"* — even through all your trials and sufferings.

Paul wrote to the Thessalonians:

> *Furthermore then we beseech you, brethren, and exhort you by the Lord Jesus, that as ye have re-ceived of us how ye ought to walk and to please God, so ye would abound more and more.*
>
> 1 Thessalonians 4:1

As you have learned to walk in God, "*abound*" in walking in that way. In other words, keep on keeping on. Persevere.

Whether you are in the Lord or not, there will be suffering. There will be trials through which you must pass. It is much better to endure your sufferings in the Lord rather than outside the Lord. Therefore, be persistent in your faith. Be persistent in your prayer life. Be persistent in your reading and meditating on the Word of God. Be persistent in your church activities and in your giving. The day is coming when you will reap — if you don't give up:

> *And let us not be weary in well doing: for in due season we shall reap, if we faint not.*
>
> Galatians 6:9

Be one of those who never faint, who don't quit. Take hold with your hands, as the spider does, and never let go. Lay hold of your spiritual life. Lay hold of your Lord. In due season, you shall reap — if you remain faithful and steadfast in God.

Another aspect of spiders is that they are creatures with patience. They can wait for hours for an insect to fly into their webs. One type of spider actually traps insects by dropping a web onto them. These must lie in wait until an insect is at just the right spot before dropping their webs.

Another type of spider makes a hole and covers

it up with a leaf or a twig, or whatever it can find. The hole is lined with webbing, making it difficult for the prey to flee. When an insect gets too near, the spider attacks it, carrying it down into its den.

All of these hunting methods take patience — patience to build the traps and patience to wait until the prey stumbles into them.

We humans are often very impatient. Once I went into a restaurant. I sat down and waited for someone to serve me. I waited five minutes, but no waiter came to take my order. I began to grow impatient. I thought, *"If he doesn't wait on me, I'm going to walk out of this place."* Well, I needed to repent for my impatience. The waiter did finally come, and I realized that he had been waiting on others who had been there before me. I had no reason to be so impatient. I hadn't fainted from hunger, after all.

Sometimes we pray with impatience. We barge into the Throne Room of God as though we are so important. We make our requests before the Lord, and then we stand back, tapping our feet, waiting impatiently for the Lord to respond in the way we want Him to. That kind of impatience leads to sin.

God has to develop patience within us. Sometimes He uses our circumstances to do this. But usually His tools are other people. Patience is often needed in dealing with relationships. When people around you aggravate you or disturb you, when you allow your anger to boil, then you need to learn patience.

We are surrounded by people, and God uses these people to test us. He wants to develop patience in us, for as we learn patience, we are becoming more like Him.

Do you want to have more patience? Then get ready for your lessons:

> *And not only so, but we glory in tribulations also: knowing that tribulation worketh patience.*
>
> Romans 5:3

If you want more patience, you will need more tribulation. The Lord will bless you to endure more trials, more suffering and more difficulties. Why? Is it because He hates you? Of course not! All these things will produce patience.

Sometimes it's your husband or your wife who will be a tribulation to you. Sometimes it may be your boss or your coworker or your pastor. Whomever God uses, whatever situation you find yourself in, be thankful that the Lord is changing you to become more like Him:

> *My brethren, count it all joy when ye fall into divers temptations; knowing this, that the trying of your faith worketh patience. But let patience have her perfect work, that ye may be perfect and entire, wanting nothing.*   James 1:2-4

Related to patience is the quality of endurance. Endurance usually refers to circumstances and difficult experiences, such as suffering, going through troubles or being mistreated. The Word of God declares:

And you will be hated by all for my name's sake.
But he who endures to the end will be saved.
                                    Matthew 10:22, NKJ

It is not enough to receive Jesus Christ. We must remain in Him. We must continue in Him and endure to the end. Then we will be saved. It is not how well we have begun that is important; it is how we finish what we have started in this life in God. Persevere. Follow through with what you have set out to do.

Sometimes we have determination, but we don't follow through. We have enough determination for today, but we have no consistency to see us through the next day. Persevere in your commitment. Have patience in your dedication. Remain steadfast in your surrender of your life to God. Hold on to Jesus Christ. Cling to Him. Abide in Him. Continue in Him.

In the Philippines, we have small lizards that live in our homes. They come in to catch insects. At night, when the insects are out flying around the lights, those house lizards are very good at catching them. They do this by walking upside down on the ceiling.

Those lizards have "stick-to-it-iveness." They know what will happen to them if they fall.

Don't let go of God. Stick with your Christian life! Many people *do* let go. That is why their lives are shattered and their dreams are lost. Don't be so easily moved, but stick with it until you reach your goal.

Is your life in God strong? Are you firm in your commitment and faith? Are you solid in your relationship with the Lord? Are you established in His grace and in His love? Are you deeply rooted in Him? If that is the case, then you can agree wholeheartedly with the apostle Paul. He said:

> *Who shall separate us from the love of Christ? shall tribulation, or distress, or persecution, or famine, or nakedness, or peril, or sword?... For I am persuaded, that neither death, nor life, nor angels, nor principalities, nor powers, nor things present, nor things to come, nor height, nor depth, nor any other creature, shall be able to separate us from the love of God, which is in Christ Jesus our Lord.* Romans 8:35, 38-39

This is steadfastness, and it is wisdom.

Let us cultivate this patience and endurance in our lives. Let us be as the spider, who "*taketh hold with her hands,*" holds on tightly and does not let go. The Word of God admonishes:

Cleaving to Your Goal

Let us hold fast the profession of our faith without wavering; (for he is faithful that promised).
Hebrews 10:23

"Hold fast" to your faith, and do not let it go. Never let go of Jesus' hand. Hold tight like a child who is crossing the street, holding tightly to his mama's hand. No matter what happens, don't let go, for He is our Security and our Protection.

The Old Testament paints a picture of this type of cleaving. The writer is describing one of David's mighty men of valor:

And after him was Eleazar the son of Dodo the Ahohite, one of the three mighty men with David, when they defied the Philistines that were there gathered together to battle, and the men of Israel were gone away: he arose, and smote the Philistines until his hand was weary, and his hand clave unto the sword: and the LORD wrought a great victory that day; and the people returned after him only to spoil.
2 Samuel 23:9-10

This Eleazar faced the enemy alone. He fought until *"his hand clave unto the sword."* In other words, he fought until the handle of the sword had gone into the flesh of his hand. Eleazar did not let go of the sword until the enemy was completely destroyed and the battle was over. He did not let go or give up. He did not quit until he had won the victory.

Hold on tight. Be steadfast. Be firm. And be faithful to do what God has entrusted to you. Victory is coming:

> *Cast thy bread upon the waters: for thou shalt find it after many days.*   Ecclesiastes 11:1

Keep on casting your bread on the waters, for victory is just around the corner. Don't give up too soon, but walk in patience, trusting the Lord. Keep your vision. Cleave to your goal.

Spiders have serious problems, and they seem to be insignificant in the face of those problems. However, they just keep climbing up higher until they find themselves in the safety of kings' palaces.

10

CLIMBING UP HIGHER

The spider ... is in kings' palaces.

Proverbs 30:28

In the last chapter, we saw that a spider "*taketh hold with her hands.*" We are to endure, to persevere, to show forth the fruit of patience in our lives. We are not to be discouraged, but to continue in faithfulness and in good works.

However, there is another part of this verse that we must look at as well. We had a glimpse of it, but now we will examine it further: "*The spider ... is in kings' palaces.*" What does this mean for us? If we are to learn from the wisdom of the spider, then we must heed her lessons.

A palace signifies a high and lofty place. It is a place of honor, royalty, dignity, glory and respect. It symbolizes power, authority, rulership and dominion. This is the position to which the lowly spider crawls.

If we are willing to learn from this small, seemingly insignificant creature, then we will come to understand that we too have a goal. We too are called upward toward a lofty position. God did not create us to remain in the dust, but to dwell in exalted places. He didn't call us to be crushed underfoot by Satan, but to climb up into a higher place — one of glory, authority and honor.

We are not subject to our situations and circumstances. They cannot control us, and they have no power over us. Instead, we can learn to control our situations.

We must refuse to submit to any situation, to any negative circumstance. We cannot always control what happens to us, but we can control our response to what happens. And most importantly, even in the most negative of circumstances, we can learn to climb ever higher.

There is a place of safety for us in God. There is a position of trusting in Him that supersedes all other positions. The psalmist found this position in God, and his words ring joyfully in truth today:

God is our refuge and strength, a very present help in trouble. Therefore will not we fear, though

*the earth be removed, and though the mountains
be carried into the midst of the sea; though the
waters thereof roar and be troubled, though the
mountains shake with the swelling thereof.*
Psalm 46:1-3

Though the earth shake violently, though the
mountains be hurled into the sea, though the waters roar and foam ... even in the midst of such
"trouble," God is our Refuge. We can run to Him and
find a place of safety. There, we can *"be still"*:

*Be still, and know that I am God: I will be exalted
among the heathen, I will be exalted in the earth.*
Psalm 46:10

Another translation of this is *"cease striving and
know." "Cease striving."* Stop struggling so much and
simply run to your place of refuge. Soar above the
circumstance. Don't let the situation consume you
with its worries and problems. Rather, renew your
strength in the Lord:

*But they that wait upon the LORD shall renew their
strength; they shall mount up with wings as ea-
gles; they shall run, and not be weary; and they
shall walk, and not faint.* Isaiah 40:31

If you feel that you are defeated, look up and find
a place of victory to which you can climb. Don't be

satisfied where you are, struggling in the midst of difficult circumstances. After all, if you are content to be poor, you may always be poor. If you are content to be sick, you may never get well. But why not climb higher? Don't be satisfied to continue keeping your eyes on your situation, when the Word of God adjures us to look to Him who is our Redeemer:

> *Looking unto Jesus the author and finisher of our faith; who for the joy that was set before him endured the cross, despising the shame, and is set down at the right hand of the throne of God.*
>
> Hebrews 12:2

Fix your eyes on Jesus and keep them there. Gaze upon Him whom your soul loves. He will guide you through whatever difficulties may come to you. He will be with you through them all, even if you cannot feel His presence. There will be times when it seems He is not there, but His love for you will give wings to your feet as you run after Him for safety.

Don't be tied too tightly to your present nest. Don't insist on staying by your old web. God will help you to make another one. When Satan is trying to crush you, when situations seem too difficult for you to bear, then why remain in the dust of this earth where your life is in danger? Why not move on up to a place where you can hold your head high without fear?

Climbing Up Higher

Climb up higher. You belong in kings' palaces. You are the child of the heavenly King, the mighty King of kings and Lord of lords.

Spiders apparently have noble aspirations. In other words, they have a strong desire to achieve something great. What about you?

Some people are satisfied just to get by in life. They are happy simply to survive from day to day, but God has better things for us. Barely making it may mean that you are still alive but simply surviving. God, however, wants you to have "*life more abundantly.*" God wants you to have a joyful life, an enjoyable life, a fulfilled life, a satisfied and victorious life. God is all you need. He is your Jehovah Jireh, the God who will provide all your needs. He is El Shaddai, the God of abundance. Let us not simply get by in life when we have such an awesome God whose desire for us is to possess everything that He has and all that He is!

The spider aspires to high places, and she is wise to do so. Even as she is spinning her web in one spot, she is spying out the land, looking for higher places to which she might later move.

Get a vision. If you have no dream of improving your life in the future, if you have no vision of rising higher in God than you are right now, then you had better settle in and get comfortable. If you have no vision, no goals, then you will achieve nothing, and you will go nowhere, and soon you will die.

But God has so much more for you. No matter where you are in your life in God, there is more for you to know, to experience, to explore, to discover and to minister to others. Raise your sights. Start moving up into the glory of the King's palace.

Perhaps you already are a person of vision. What are you doing to make that dream a reality? Are you spying out the higher ground? Are you looking for ways to elevate your situation? Are you getting ready to scale the heights? Are you running the race? Are you pressing on? Are you desiring for more of God?

Maybe some would call yours "the impossible dream." For them, perhaps it is, but for those of us who love God, there is no impossible dream. Our dream is the attainable dream. We can do it through Christ:

> *I can do all things through Christ who strengthens me.*   Philippians 4:13, NKJ

> *Jesus said unto him, If thou canst believe, all things are possible to him that believeth.*
>   Mark 9:23

You can accomplish great things in God. Move on up into His glory. Move on up into a place where nothing disturbs, where nothing harms, where no one can rob you of the blessing of God.

Move on up. What is holding you back? Whatever it is, you can overcome it through the power of the Holy Spirit.

Dream and keep on dreaming. Dream without shame, and keep your dream alive.

Dreams can seem such fragile things. They can be broken so easily if they are not carefully guarded. Careless words of friends, the gnawings of self-doubt, the mocking of enemies ... all of these are the enemies of dreams. But if a dream is not nurtured, it will die. Cultivate and nourish your God-given dreams. Guard them wisely, and look to see the ways in which they will come to pass. Put life into action and let it help you find your fulfillment in God.

Spiders' webs, too, are fragile. They seem so delicate, so easy to destroy. Yet the webs themselves are made of one of the strongest known substances.

Do you have something worth fighting for? I believe you do. You have your faith in the Lord Jesus. You have the dreams, the visions and the goals that He has given you. You have the special part that only you can play in your local church and in your local community, helping to usher in the Kingdom of God. Yes, you have something worth fighting for. Never give up, never look back and never let go of your dreams. Keep pushing and pressing on. Keep running the race. Keep looking forward toward the finish line where you will receive your crown of victory. Remember, the King's palace awaits you. Jesus said:

Let not your heart be troubled: ye believe in God, believe also in me. In my Father's house are many mansions: if it were not so, I would have told you. I go to prepare a place for you. And if I go and prepare a place for you, I will come again, and receive you unto myself; that where I am, there ye may be also. John 14:1-3

Come up higher. God has more for you. His purpose for you is not to be mired in difficulty and doubts. He longs for you to reach out to Him, as He reaches out to you. So come up higher, by fixing your mind and thoughts on Him. Be a man or a woman of the Word; be faithful in prayer, and have confidence in your faith and in the power of God.

Yes, there will still be problems. God never promised that we would escape the difficulties of life. In fact, Christ has promised the opposite. There will be "*tribulation*" for us, but let us look at the second part of that promise.

These things I have spoken unto you, that in me ye might have peace. In the world ye shall have tribulation: but be of good cheer; I have overcome the world. John 16:33

Life won't become easy just because we have given our lives over to the Lord, but if there were no problems to overcome, we could not be overcomers!

Climbing Up Higher

If you are considering giving up, think about the spider. She works to attain a place in an earthly palace, one that will eventually crumble, but we are working toward an eternal reward. The palace we seek can never decay. It is not made of fine wood or marble. The city in which we will one day dwell is a city *"whose builder and maker is God."*

We can keep moving up higher as long as we are living here on earth. Our problems and trials can be a ladder on which we move ever upward.

One day we will make the most important move of all. The trumpet will sound, and we will make a permanent move into the presence of God. For now, we can keep moving up, coming ever closer to the goal.

So don't give up now. You have come too far to turn back. You are closer to the goal than ever before. Keep moving up, for the goal is in sight. And soon you will hear Him say, *"Well done thou good and faithful servant; enter thou into the joy of thy Lord."*

Did you know that God has His goals too — things that He wants to accomplish in your life? He does, and He is working to bring them about in you:

> *Being confident of this very thing, that he which hath begun a good work in you will perform it until the day of Jesus Christ.*   Philippians 1:6

God will never cease working until He has perfected you and accomplished His purposes in your life. Don't hinder His work in you. Don't be satisfied with less than what He has prepared for you. Be willing to follow Him, and to be raised up higher.

In moving her web, the spider does not simply change her place of work. She doesn't just stay in the web for a shift and then go home. Whenever she moves her web, she is changing her dwelling place, her home.

Whenever we move up to a higher realm in God, this doesn't imply that it's just for Sunday mornings or a few meetings through the week. When we climb higher — which is to say, whenever we experience and minister more of the presence of God in our lives — that place becomes our residence. We dwell there. We remain there continually, at least until we move to the next higher place the Lord shows us:

> *But we all, with open face beholding as in a glass the glory of the Lord, are changed into the same image from glory to glory, even as by the Spirit of the Lord.* 2 Corinthians 3:18

Allow yourself to move into the things of God, being changed *"from glory to glory"* into the image of the Son, Christ Jesus.

Some of that changing will be through trials and testings, but we can take heart and be encouraged as we allow the Scriptures to take root in our hearts:

Climbing Up Higher

For which cause we faint not; but though our outward man perish, yet the inward man is renewed day by day. For our light affliction, which is but for a moment, worketh for us a far more exceeding and eternal weight of glory; while we look not at the things which are seen, but at the things which are not seen: for the things which are seen are temporal; but the things which are not seen are eternal.　　2 Corinthians 4:16-18

What a beautiful word from the Lord! Even though we go through trials and suffering, even though we may be weakened outwardly, yet our inward man *"is renewed day by day."* And the things we suffer now are *"but for a moment."* They are temporary, even though it sometimes seems as though they go on forever. But they are for our benefit, since they work in us *"a far more exceeding and eternal weight of glory."*

When you are about to give up because of your suffering, think about the glory that is awaiting you. Think of the smile on the face of the Master as He waits for you in glory.

Come up higher, my friend. Fix your eyes on your Lord and rise above all those things that would drag you down. Come up higher to the place of refuge, to the place of safety.

Come up higher. Learn the wisdom of the spider.

PART SIX:

LIVING THE OVERCOMING LIFE

11

PROBLEMS TOO BIG TO FACE?

And [Goliath] *stood and cried unto the armies of Israel. ... And David was the youngest.*

1 Samuel 17:8 and 14

Like the four small creatures we have looked at, we sometimes feel small and insignificant. Sometimes it's hard to be like the spider, climbing above our difficulties to find peace in God. Sometimes it's hard to prepare for the days ahead as the ant does. We are having enough trouble just getting through today. And sometimes it seems that we will never get in step with those around us. We cannot be locusts, for we're too busy stumbling around to march to the correct beat.

Sometimes the only one of these creatures we can identify with is the coney — the creature who knows his own weakness.

At times we tend to feel that we cannot accomplish what God has asked us to do, and we always seem to think how much better qualified others seem to be to do the things God has asked of us.

Sometimes it's easy to feel unimportant. "After all," you might say, "I'm just a homemaker." "I'm just a Sunday school teacher." "I'm just a mechanic." But how do you know how God will use your mechanical abilities, or how you will minister to the next customer who walks into your shop? How do you know what God will do with the lives of your children? Can you envision the ways in which He wants to use your home as a place of outreach and ministry? Do you really perceive what God will do in the lives of those you are teaching or training?

The Bible tells the story of a young man who seemed to others to be insignificant. His own brothers looked down on him. Even his father forgot to call him when he was asked to present his sons before the prophet. He didn't seem to be important, but God didn't agree with this opinion.

David was a shepherd, tending his father's flocks. He was "just" David, "just" the shepherd, "just" the youngest of his father's sons. He was nothing much, nothing special.

One day David was sent by his father to carry

messages and food to his brothers, who were in the army of Saul, king of Israel. There he saw a giant who challenged the people of God:

And he stood and cried unto the armies of Israel, and said unto them, Why are ye come out to set your battle in array? am not I a Philistine, and ye servants to Saul? choose you a man for you, and let him come down to me. If he be able to fight with me, and to kill me, then will we be your servants: but if I prevail against him, and kill him, then shall ye be our servants, and serve us. And the Philistine said, I defy the armies of Israel this day; give me a man, that we may fight together.

1 Samuel 17:8-10

Goliath saw no need for the two armies to fight. All Israel needed to do was to come up with a champion to face him. But then, Goliath was ... Goliath! He was the champion, the giant, a trained and experienced fighter. As far as he could see, he had no cause for concern.

The warriors in Saul's army were terrified of the man. They trembled in fear at the challenge. Goliath was more than nine feet tall. His looks were imposing, to say the least. Everyone was afraid to face him. Saul's best warriors were saying: "This giant is too great and too mighty to face. Compared to him, we are nothing."

Then came David, the young shepherd, whose life was playing his harp and tending his father's sheep. He had come on his father's errand to meet his brothers, and to see how the battle went. The problem was that there was no battle. There was only the challenge of the giant.

When David heard the challenge of the Philistine, he grew very angry. He saw things a little differently than the cowering army of Saul did. He didn't look at his own insignificance. Instead, he looked to his God. And David said, "I'll go and face this uncircumcised Philistine. Who does he think he is? Compared to the great and mighty God of Israel, he is nothing!"

He is nothing! What is it in your life that seems so difficult to face? Is there a Goliath lurking somewhere, threatening to conquer you? Perhaps you look at that thing and say, "Oh, it is too big to face! I can't deal with this! I can't walk in victory in this circumstance!" Well, take a lesson from David. Don't look at your own seeming insignificance and your lack of ability. Look to God's ability. And don't be sidetracked by those who would point out to you your lack. For David, it was his brothers who tried to help him see that he could not possibly face the giant:

And David spake to the men that stood by him, saying, What shall be done to the man that killeth this Philistine, and taketh away the reproach from Israel? for who is this uncircumcised Philistine, that he should defy the armies of the living God? And the people answered him after this manner, saying, So shall it be done to the man that killeth him. And Eliab his eldest brother heard when he spake unto the men; and Eliab's anger was kindled against David, and he said, Why camest thou down hither? and with whom hast thou left those few sheep in the wilderness? I know thy pride, and the naughtiness of thine heart; for thou art come down that thou mightest see the battle.

1 Samuel 17:26-28

David's brothers said to him, "Go on home. You are too proud. You always want to show off. Go back and tend our father's sheep. There is nothing you can do here. Can't you see he's a giant? Don't you realize that he's too big to face?"

David said, "I can face this giant. What is he? He is just an uncircumcised Philistine, taunting the armies of the living God."

The young man was brought before King Saul. This was not the first time Saul had met David. The king already knew him, for he had been summoned as a musician to soothe Saul when his spirit was troubled. He came highly recommended:

Then answered one of the servants, and said, Be-

*hold, I have seen a son of Jesse the Bethlehemite,
that is cunning in playing, and a mighty valiant
man, and a man of war, and prudent in matters,
and a comely person, and the LORD is with him.*

1 Samuel 16:18

Saul liked what he witnessed in the young David:

*And David came to Saul, and stood before him:
and he loved him greatly; and he became his
armourbearer. And Saul sent to Jesse, saying, Let
David, I pray thee, stand before me; for he hath
found favour in my sight.*   1 Samuel 16:21-22

Saul probably believed he had David's best interest at heart when he tried to influence him not to face Goliath. But David asked, "Is there anyone here among you who would go?" Of course there was none, since all the soldiers had been running in fear from the giant for the past forty days. So again David decided to face the unfaceable, looking without wincing at the giant.

David did some more comparing, but again he didn't look at his seeming insignificance, but remembered the wild beasts he had slain as he guarded the flocks of his father. David said to Saul:

*Thy servant slew both the lion and the bear: and
this uncircumcised Philistine shall be as one of*

*them, seeing he hath defied the armies of the liv-
ing God. David said moreover, The* LORD *that de-
livered me out of the paw of the lion, and out of
the paw of the bear, he will deliver me out of the
hand of this Philistine. And Saul said unto David,
Go, and the* LORD *be with thee.*

1 Samuel 17:36-37

Saul tried to prepare David to meet the giant by
loaning him his own armor. David tried it on, but it
was too large for him, too heavy for him to carry.
How could he fight when he could barely move?
The armor that was well able to protect Saul when
he went into battle could do nothing for David, because it did not fit his situation.

When you are called into battle, when you must
face that thing that seems too terrible to face, that is
not the time to accept someone else's armor. Well-
meaning people may try to press their armor upon
you, thinking it will help you. But, like David, you
must rely on the defenses the Lord has given you.
You must recall the battles He has already helped
you to win. Most importantly, you must look to your
God and know that He can meet any challenge in
your life. It is not the weapons of man that will see
you through, but the power of the Spirit of God.

So David took off all the armor of the king. He
knew that he would not be able to win the victory if
he trusted in *"the arm of flesh."* And all the while,

everyone around him was saying, "But David, look at him! That giant Goliath is too big to face! You will be killed, and we will all be enslaved. He is just too big!"

Think about your biggest problem, your greatest fear. Think of how it immobilizes you as it seems to grow to block out all other concerns. Perhaps you have refused to face the problem, leaving it until later. But it seems never to leave, only to grow. Now, think about David's attitude.

David looked around at all the people who were trying to discourage him. He looked at Goliath. He looked back to his past victories. And he looked to his God. And David proclaimed boldly, "No! This giant is not too big to face! That is not what I see. Look again. He is too big to miss! In the name of the Lord, I will destroy him. This giant is too big to miss."

God is bigger than all our problems, than all our cares, than all of our needs. Our God is greater than all those things that surround us and that threaten to overtake us. Ours is the God of the impossible. He is the God of the supernatural. He is able to do *"exceeding abundantly above all that we ask or think, according to the power that worketh in us."*

We must begin to move from our natural self-consciousness into a spiritual consciousness in God. We must begin to see ourselves the way God sees us, the way we should be according to His Word. And we need to come out of our fears, our unbelief and our discouragement, stepping into the supernatural things of God. We must begin to look at things as David did if we are to become giant-slayers. We should not compare ourselves to the enemy.

So David, having taken off the armor of Saul, having laid aside what man thought would be best, picked up his slingshot. He went down to a brook to choose five small, smooth stones. They seemed quite insignificant. But with them he went out to face the giant.

David seemed so puny, so insignificant, that Goliath was insulted when the lad was sent out against him. "*Am I a dog,*" he raved, "*that you would send out such a one to fight me with his stick?*" Goliath cursed David by the names of his gods. He taunted David, but the shepherd turned the mocking back upon the head of the giant. David proclaimed the name of his God, so that all would know whose victory it really was:

> *Then said David to the Philistine, Thou comest to me with a sword, and with a spear, and with a shield: but I come to thee in the name of the LORD of hosts, the God of the armies of Israel, whom thou hast defied. This day will the LORD deliver thee into mine hand ... that all the earth may know that there is a God in Israel. And all this assembly shall know that the LORD saveth not with*

175

sword and spear: for the battle is the LORD*'s, and he will give you into our hands.*

1 Samuel 17:45-47

When Goliath came up to meet him, David was ready. He took a stone from his leather bag, placed it in the sling and began to swing it. He did not allow himself to be intimidated by the giant, nor did he see himself as being insignificant in the face of his enemy. He did not ponder the possibility of failure. This Philistine had taunted the armies of the living God. He had set himself against God Almighty. So how could David just stand by and allow him to continue? No! He had to be dealt with. And, since no one else could be found to do it, David would.

Goliath was about to learn a hard lesson: with God there are no insignificant people, and in God there is no impossibility.

As Goliath came forward to meet David, that young man ran toward him, swinging his weapon. The stone flew, and the giant fell.

Saul's army went wild with rejoicing. David had won the victory for the entire nation with one small, seemingly insignificant stone. It had become a powerful weapon. A small stone released into the hand of God was powerful to accomplish a divine purpose.

Face your situation. Look at that problem that has you cowering in fear and worry. Then look to your

God. Swing your slingshot of faith, and say to your problem, "You are not too big to face. You are too big to miss. And in the name of the Lord Jesus Christ, I will destroy you!" Then, in the Spirit of the Lord, do it.

As you do, you will see the power of God at work in your life. When you begin to take steps of faith, you are moving out of the natural and into the supernatural. Then things begin to happen in the heavenlies. If you will place all your weaknesses, all your inabilities, all your lacks in the hand of God, He can turn your situation around in a moment's time.

And when that happens, you suddenly gain importance in the eyes of those around you. They suddenly realize what God knew all along: that you are important in the Kingdom of God, and that you can make a difference. They begin to see that power of God at work in your life, just as you have begun to see it. Are you glorified as a result? No! God is glorified for what He can do with one person's life.

Don't ever belittle yourself or underestimate what you can do in God. God loves to take the small things, the seemingly unimportant people, and use them to His glory. Paul wrote about this:

> *Because the foolishness of God is wiser than men; and the weakness of God is stronger than men. For ye see your calling, brethren, how that not many wise men after the flesh, not many mighty,*

not many noble, are called: but God hath chosen the foolish things of the world to confound the wise; and God hath chosen the weak things of the world to confound the things which are mighty; and base things of the world, and things which are despised, hath God chosen, yea, and things which are not, to bring to nought things that are: that no flesh should glory in his presence.

1 Corinthians 1:25-29

When something is accomplished that we know we could not do on our own, we give God the glory. We attribute all success to Him. All the glory is His. This is how we are to live our lives: bringing God glory, recognizing His working through us. But we cannot do this when we are paralyzed by fear, hiding behind the common sense that tells us we cannot move out in the things of God.

Sometimes it is difficult to begin to do what God is telling us to do, whether it be preaching, evangelizing the lost or simply making ours a home of hospitality where others can be free to come for ministry and healing. But we must be faithful if we are to accomplish the purpose and destiny God has set in place in our lives. Sometimes we need to renew our minds through the promises of God:

If thou canst believe, all things are possible

178

Problems Too Big to Face?

to him that believeth.   Mark 9:23

Greater is he that is in you, than he that is in the world.   1 John 4:4

If God be for us, who can be against us?
           Romans 8:31

Not by might, nor by power, but by my Spirit, saith the LORD *of hosts.*   Zechariah 4:6

For as many of you as have been baptized into Christ have put on Christ.   Galatians 3:27

No weapon that is formed against thee shall prosper; and every tongue that shall rise against thee in judgment thou shalt condemn. This is the heritage of the servants of the LORD, *and their righteousness is of me, saith the* LORD.
           Isaiah 54:17

For the weapons of our warfare are not carnal, but mighty through God to the pulling down of strong holds.   2 Corinthians 10:4

Behold, I give unto you power to tread on serpents and scorpions, and over all the power of the enemy: and nothing shall by any means hurt you.
           Luke 10:19

If you will accept these promises of God and begin to act on them, a whole new world will be opened to you. As you accept what God has to say, you can begin to see yourself as God sees you, as His Word describes you. Work toward the goal of becoming what God has designed you to be.

Whatever the hindrance to fulfilling your purpose in God, whatever the problem, God is greater. Put your life in the hands of the Lord. Let Him fill you with His power and anointing. Allow Him to release you to move and flow in the power of God. And you'll never be the same.

Don't limit yourself, because your God is unlimited. Whatever the problem, it is not too big to face. It is too big to miss.

12

No Longer Without Purpose

But we preach Christ crucified, unto the Jews a stumblingblock, and unto the Greeks foolishness; but unto them which are called, both Jews and Greeks, Christ the power of God, and the wisdom of God. Because the foolishness of God is wiser than men; and the weakness of God is stronger than men. For ye see your calling, brethren, how that not many wise men after the flesh, not many mighty, not many noble, are called: but God hath chosen the foolish things of the world to confound the wise; and God hath chosen the weak things of the world to confound the things which are mighty; and base things of the world, and things which are despised, hath God chosen, yea, and things which are not, to bring to nought things that are: that no flesh should glory in his presence. 1 Corinthians 1:23-29

The ant, the coney, the locust, the spider ... yes, God has indeed chosen *"the foolish things of the world"* for our instruction. These are four small creatures and many would say that they are unimportant. But as we have seen, they may be small, but they are also wise.

Since the Bible holds up these four seemingly insignificant creatures as examples to us, we want to adopt the wisdom and the principles we see at work in them. If we despise them, we will show ourselves foolish. If we consider them carefully, taking to heart their lessons, we can become wise.

We take many ordinary things for granted, considering them to be of little value. But there is much to be gained by considering some of the seemingly ordinary things in our lives. Listen for what the Spirit of the Lord is saying through the seemingly small, everyday things of your life.

The Bible shows us that God speaks through the mundane. Christ spoke of the grass, the flowers, the birds, and of tasks as simple and common as making bread and planting seeds. The Spirit of the Lord spoke to Jeremiah as he watched a clay vessel being formed on the potter's wheel, and He even spoke to him through the example of a new belt.

So allow yourself to hear the Lord speaking to your heart. Ask Him what He would say to you. Tune your spiritual ears to hear His voice. And then heed what you hear.

Be inspired by these four creatures. Be challenged by them. Dare to apply the wisdom that has made them significant in God's eyes.

Learn from the ant.

Learn from the coney.

Learn from the locust.

And learn the wisdom of the spider.

Though they are all weak, they have much to teach us.

If you are powerless, that is not a problem. God will give you His power. If you are not well-educated, that is not a problem. God will help you to learn.

I am sure that I have not fully accomplished all that God has for me to do. I know that I have a long way to go, but I also know that I have come a long way already and that God has done great things in my life. I am not satisfied; I have a desire to do greater things for God.

Be glad that you are who God created you to be. Don't look down on yourself.

Once I was trying to change a light bulb in my house. The room where the bulb needed to be replaced has a high ceiling, and I'm not very tall. Since I had no ladder, I got a chair. But when I stood on top of the chair, I still couldn't reach the light fixture. I put a dictionary on the chair and tried again, but I still couldn't reach it. I added the telephone book, but I was still too short.

By this time I was getting frustrated! I was so disgusted with myself that I said, "Oh, why did God create me to be so short? If I was only a little bit taller, I wouldn't be frustrated trying to change this light bulb. It would be a simple thing."

Then the Holy Spirit began to speak in my heart, saying, "I am happy with you just the way you are. I take pleasure and delight in you."

And the Lord says the same to you today. He takes great pleasure and delight in you the way you are. God has created you as He saw fit. Enjoy His gift to you, appreciate it, welcome it. God has created us each different and unique, so that we can complement one another in His Kingdom.

God has a work designed just for you. And whatever that work is, He has created you in such a way that you can do it. He will give you the talents and giftings you need. He will give you the ability, the power and the creative energy you need to be able to fulfill His calling upon your life. He is God! He knows what you need to be able to obey His word to you. But be certain that you know this: God has a purpose for you.

No Longer Insignificant

No matter who you are, no matter how you think of yourself or how those around you think of you, God created you for a specific purpose. And that purpose is far more important than you can possibly imagine.

How do you see yourself? Who are you in God? What do you want to do in His Kingdom? Much of what you do in the Kingdom depends on you. It depends on your level of commitment. It depends on your willingness to surrender your life to Christ. It depends upon your living your life in a holy and godly manner, acknowledging Him as your Lord.

God has a purpose for you. The devil will try his best to keep you from fulfilling it. But you can be what you want to be if you determine in your heart to be what God has purposed you to be.

How can you do this? Let God be God in you. Let His life flow through you, and out to others as you minister to them. You can be what God intended you to be if you allow God to be what He wants to be in your life. When you allow Him to be God in your life, and to express Himself supernaturally through you, then you will be transformed in God from an ordinary to an extraordinary person.

We should be living in such a way as to please God and bring honor and glory to Him. Our lives should show forth the life of Christ within us, glorifying Him. As our lives become reflections of His life, we will find our purpose.

So learn the wisdom of these insignificant creatures. Look to the Lord to find your purpose in life. And allow Him to fulfill that purpose in you.

No matter how insignificant you may seem to others, God wants to make you His dwelling place, to shine in you His glory. Then, when the Creator of the universe, the God of all creation, can manifest Himself through you, and the God of the impossible, the One who holds this world together, dwells in you, you can only imagine what can be accomplished. Therefore, let go and let God make you what He wants you to be.

God created us in His image. All that He is is in us. Unleash that power, and you will find your true purpose — in Him.

Amen!

There be four things which are little upon the earth, but they are exceeding wise: the ants are a people not strong, yet they prepare their meat in the summer; the conies are but a feeble folk, yet make they their houses in the rocks; the locusts have no king, yet go they forth all of them by bands; the spider taketh hold with her hands, and is in kings' palaces. Proverbs 30:24-28

Another great book by Ray Llarena:

Founded on the ROCK

Finding God's Order for Your Family

- *Is your marriage all that you hoped it would be?*
- *Is raising your children more of a challenge than you expected?*
- *Is the atmosphere of your home as pleasing to the Lord as you would like it to be?*
- *Does your family life reflect the character expected of believers?*

If you are uncertain about your answers to these questions, you are in good company. The Christian marriage and the Christian home are under a concerted attack by the enemy of our souls — all over the world, and we all need God's help to overcome this attack. This book, a result of years of marriage counseling, special seminars for the family and a world of personal experience, has practical answers to the questions that have plagued many Christian families in recent years.

Perfect bound. 210 pages. ISBN 1-884369-12-X   *$12.99*

Principles of Christian Faith
A Bible Study Series for Laying Foundations in Spirit-Filled Believers

by Harold McDougal

- *What do we, as spirit-filled Christians, believe?*
- *Can we put our beliefs into meaningful words?*
- *Can we teach what we believe to others?*

Here is a book that has been used by thousands of believers on several continents to prepare men and women for life and for the work of the Lord. It is unsurpassed in simplicity, yet it lays a full biblical foundation. It has been used successfully not only in ministerial training programs, but in home Bible study groups, in prison ministry outreaches and to teach new believers everywhere. This is an enlarged and improved edition of the original book.

Perfect bound. 344 pages. ISBN 1-884369-66-9   *$17.99*

Speaking in Tongues
The Uses and Abuses of this Supernatural Phenomenon

by Harold McDougal

Millions of people around the world are experiencing this very strange phenomenon. Why? And what, if anything, should they do next?

- *What is speaking in tongues?*
- *What is the purpose of speaking in tongues?*
- *Why is this such a controversial subject?*
- *Will speaking in tongues do anything for me personally?*
- *Does God expect everyone to speak in tongues?*

Here is a book written in everyday language that clearly answers these and many other questions people everywhere ask about speaking in tongues, a book that will show you how to unlock the spiritual treasures God is offering to His Church in these last days.

Perfect bound. 140 pages. ISBN 1-884369-07-3   *$10.99*

Empowered for the Call
Understanding the Dynamics of the Anointing

by Tim Bagwell

"*Empowered for the Call* plumbs the depth and breadth of God's anointing power and is a valuable addition to every Christian's library."   — *Dr. Oral Roberts*

"I highly recommend this relevant and timely message to all those who desire truth. It lays down principles that are destined to impact your life and the world around you."   — *Dr. Myles Munroe*

"This powerful work will revolutionize the reader's concept of the anointing."   — *Dr. Larry Lea*

"Tim Bagwell dares to put into manuscript form God's challenging concepts on the anointing."

— *Dr. Ralph Wilkerson*

"Tim Bagwell is once again on the cutting edge with this much-needed book. He has captured the essence of all that is inherent in the anointing power of God."

— *Evangelist Tim Storey*

Perfect bound. 168 pages. ISBN 1-884369-73-1 $10.99

Ministry address:

PASTOR RAY LLARENA
Harvest Center
4554 N Broadway
Suite 228
Chicago, IL 60613

Printed in the USA
CPSIA information can be obtained
at www.ICGtesting.com
JSHW081007220224
57650JS00001B/5